The Little Book Of
LIVER BIRDS

David Cottrell

LIVERPOOL
1207~2007

The Little Book Of
LIVER BIRDS

David Cottrell

breedon **books**
PUBLISHING

First published in Great Britain in 2006 by
The Breedon Books Publishing Company Limited
Breedon House, 3 The Parker Centre, Derby DE21 4SZ.

Reprinted in 2008

ISBN 1 85983 547 3
ISBN13 978-1-85983-547-0

Printed and bound in China

CONTENTS

For my family. My love to thee.

Without whom...

Thanks to the ever-helpful staff at National Museums
Liverpool, Central Library Record Office, the University of
Liverpool's Sydney Jones Library and the Town Hall, those
who greased the wheels at Merseyside Fire Museum, Royal
Insurance, Barclays Bank, Grosvenor plc, Liverpool Football
Club, St George's Hall, Ogdens and Picton Road Baths, and
the too-numerous-to-mention caretakers and concierges
who opened the doors to secret rooms, windswept rooftops
and harrying seagulls. Once the idea for this book was
conceived, its inspiration and motivation were consistently
the wonderful everyday people of Liverpool whose
generosity, enthusiasm and pride in their city obliged its
completion. Don't ever doubt it, this is a special place.

All photography by the author except:
p18 National Trust; p23 Liverpool Record Office;
p36 (bottom left) Julian Greene; p39 (portrait) National Trust;
p131 NMR / English Heritage.

'We have something no zoo has ever seen, no museums have ever secured, nor the world's wealth can buy — the Liver Bird'
Eric Hardy, Liverpool Review, July 1934

Sailors' Home gates

HERE, THERE AND EVERYWHERE

Late in 2004, a couple of months after Liverpool had been officially inscribed as a UNESCO World Heritage Site, construction workers made a dramatic discovery on the site of Grosvenor's £750 million Paradise Street redevelopment — an artefact that, for many local historians and archaeologists, was as thrilling as Howard Carter's excavations in the Valley of the Kings.

Close to the waterfront on Canning Place they unearthed decorative carvings from a celebrated Sailors' Home opened in 1850 and demolished in 1973. Face down in the rubble was a familiar creature of modern mythology, measuring 4ft tall and sculpted in relief from red sandstone on a large, circular base: the eagle-eyed Liver Bird, with its wings at rest and seaweed clutched in its bill, which had stood guard over the six-storey building's mock-Jacobean entrance during Liverpool's zenith as one of the world's greatest ports, and then lain forgotten on derelict land for three bleak decades.

Sailors Home entablature

Already moves had been made to return the Home's magnificent iron gates from a West Midlands foundry. Over 15ft high and decorated with mermaids and sea serpents, oars and rigging, hooks and tillers, horns and shells, they had been cast in 1840 by the Liverpool foundry Henry Pooley & Son but transferred south after the firm moved premises to Smethwick. Their centrepiece was a gilded Liver Bird, again with lowered wings, beneath a crown. Like the sandstone sculpture, it pre-dated its famous cousins on top of the Royal Liver Building by at least 60 years.

By early 2005, another bird — this one brand new — had made Liverpool's headlines

Tracey Emin's
Roman Standard

Lamp standard, William Brown Street

Entrance, Martins Bank Building

when artist Tracey Emin unveiled her first piece of public art. Entitled *Roman Standard* and perched upon a tall, bronze pole near to the massive Anglican Cathedral, it paid homage to the city's wealth of neoclassical architecture. The creature resembled a swift rather than a Liver Bird, but Emin's sentiments struck a chord. 'Birds are the angels of this world,' she declared.

In which case, Liverpool must be its little corner of heaven. Nowhere in Britain – nor perhaps on the planet – can such prolific sentinels be found. They roost not just upon iconic waterfront office buildings, but on old banks and hotels, museums and libraries, factories and warehouses, schools and colleges, shops and pubs, hospitals and fire stations. Over the years they have colonised cemeteries, bridges, lamp-posts, bollards and even public bins and toilets.

Their bodies are not flesh and blood but stone, brick, iron, bronze, brass, glass, enamel, clay and wood, rendered as sculpture, statuary, paintings and mosaics in every shade of colour. They stand proud or timid, serene or excitable, elegant or scruffy, fat or thin, plausible or preposterous.

For the Liver Bird is an authentic Liverpudlian chimera, a Scouse griffin borne from unbridled imagination, and a creature of protean forms and composite pieces. Part legendary roc or phoenix and part dodo – almost extinct but still very much alive, it is impossibly proportioned and wonderfully ludicrous: the hefty chest and shaggy plumage of an ostrich or emu, for instance, supported by an eagle's powerful wings and legs ending in a duck's dainty webbed feet, with a peacock's flamboyant tail, the graceful looped neck of a swan, long slender bill of a heron and fanciful crest of a grebe.

In turn its wings are elevated or folded, with both feet firmly on the ground – usually a sinewy wreath – or one foot raised with pomp. Invariably, but not always, it carries a singular sprig of seaweed in its bill. Upon Liverpool's customary coat of arms it appears three times, above and inside a crest and within a flag carried by Neptune. Elsewhere it nests in shields and shells amid nautical motifs, fabulous creatures of the deep, majestic crowns and Latin mottos. And as a rule it faces to the left, although it can be found full-frontal and even depicted overhead.

Only, of course, if you look. Conspicuous to most visitors yet invisible to many natives, these Liver Birds bear silent witness to the spectacular rise, rapid fall and timely renaissance of the city. They have seen the ebb and flow of its fortunes, the coming and going of its people, and the countless acts – great and small, wise and foolish played out upon its changing landscape – even as their own numbers dwindle in an age when traditional architectural decoration has become obsolete.

Collectively they are redolent of a very different Liverpool from recent years, a cryptic emblem of an older, glorious metropolis of almost one million inhabitants that was planned and built by a nascent, liberal-minded middle class. A century ago, no building or monument of worth in Liverpool was complete without this mythical motif inspired by classical sculpture, symbolising the power and prosperity, civic pride and self-regard of the British Empire's greatest port.

Times have changed, but many Liver Birds have survived in a city that, until recently, was an anaemic incarnation of its former self. Those that still linger, by luck or design, tell something of Liverpool's unique story as it celebrates its 800th birthday and status as European Capital of Culture in 2008.

Bronze door grille, St George's Hall

A CORMORANT TO ARMS

Take an eagle that looks like a dove. Transform it into a cormorant. Give it a new title borrowed from a Dutch term for a duck that sounds a bit like an old word for seaweed and the first half of a city's name. Invent the Liver Bird.

So received opinion has it, but the origins of Liverpool's famous symbol remain contentious. Let's start with the heraldic description of the city's coat of arms, granted as late as 1797...

'The Dexter [to observer's left] Neptune, with his sea-green mantle [cloak] flowing, the waist wreathed with Laver [seaweed]; on his head an Eastern crown gold; in the right hand his trident sable [black]; the left supporting a banner of the arms of Liverpool; on the sinister [right] a triton, wreathed as the dexter, and blowing his shell; the right hand supporting a banner, thereon a ship under sail in perspective all proper the banner-staves Or [gold or yellow]... Argent [silver], a Cormorant, in the beak a branch of seaweed called Laver, and, for the Crest, on a wreath of the colours, a Cormorant, the wings elevated, in the beak a branch of Laver; the motto is Deus Nobis Haec Otia Fecit'.

The motto comes from the *Eclogues of Virgil*, a series of poems about an idyllic landscape called Arcadia, and translates as: 'These comforts/gifts God has bestowed upon us'. A fitting epigram for an opulent and ideal-istic young city which, as we shall see,

Armorial bearings, 1794 (left) and 1890

embraced the classical world's values in the 19th century.

Reportedly, the cormorant beat off competition from a galleon in full sail, seahorses and an elephant's tusk to be ratified on the arms. Local historian J. Wall, whose *Quest for the Liver Bird* was published by the Historical Society of Lancashire and Cheshire in 1967, claimed that the use of the word 'laver' (from the Latin for edible seaweed) in the heraldic description 'is an instance of what the Heralds call a canting or punning allusion to the name of the town'. But, he adds, 'most writers on the subject are mistaken, it seems to me, in regarding the bird itself in the same light... the cormorant only became known as a liver bird after it was adopted for Liverpool's badge, and not before'.

In fact, when Liverpool dignitary Clayton Tarleton wrote to the College of Arms in 1796 to apply for the grant, he described the bird as 'a lever or sea cormorant'. And, as far back as 1668, a heraldic scholar named Randle Holme III recorded the Earl of Derby presenting a silver mace 'engraved with... the arms of the town, viz, a leaver'.

So, contrary to J. Wall's assumption, 'lever' or 'leaver' does appear to have been in common usage as an alternative name for the cormorant by the 18th century. The same Randle Holme III could well be the culprit. Its roots, he revealed, lay in the Low Dutch word 'lepler' or 'lefler' that actually means shoveler duck or spoonbill. The National Museums Liverpool (NML) Maritime Archives & Library claims that this is 'a clear case of false associations — a confusion of the cormorant with the shoveler and spoonbill, so as to make the emblematic bird's name a play on the name Liverpool!'

It adds that the Liver Bird 'is part of Liverpool's modern, rather than ancient, folklore' and that the copper creatures crowning the Royal Liver Building 'helped to fix in the popular mind the myth that the Liver was a fabulous bird that once haunted the Pool inlet'. William Enfield's *History of Liverpool*, published in 1774, corroborates this view, declaring that the bird — whatever its label — existed only 'in fabulous tradition and the Herald's office'.

The name Liverpool has equally ambiguous origins. One theory derives it from the Old English 'lifrig' meaning 'thick with water'. *A New Illustrated Guide to Liverpool*, originally published in 1902 and since reissued by the city's Central Library, begs to differ and quotes James Picton, a famous Victorian architect and Liverpool historian, in its case: 'The curious bird, holding a piece of seaweed in its bill, has been the cause of much controversy... Sir J.A. Picton says, "The Liver was a foolish invention to account for the name. There was the Pool, which accounted for the last syllable, and there was the bird on the seal or shield which, in the absence of other information, was supposed to indicate the prefix."

'He also states that undoubtedly the word has its true origin in the Welsh Llivr — "Confluence" — and Pwll — obviously "Pool" — so that the whole word means, "the expanse at the pool" or "the pool at the confluence." So here we have this nondescript bird — in reality, Sir J.A. Picton says, "an immature cormorant" (a stuffed specimen of which is to be seen at the Town Hall) — occupying this proud position to which it does not appear to be justly entitled.'

Young (above) and adult cormorant specimens, World Museum Liverpool

That stuffed specimen is now held in the vaults of World Museum Liverpool, along with an adult cormorant. It has been alleged that the former bird was sent to the College of Arms in 1796 but it probably dates to 1860 at the earliest, while the mature cormorant was stuffed in the early 20th century.

Even so, it is not too fatuous to assume that the species – which, incidentally, does not eat seaweed – was a prominent fixture along the Mersey up to 200 years ago when increasing industrial pollution may have begun to drive it away. In today's cleaner environment it roosts in great numbers at Seaforth Nature Reserve, an area of 30 hectares at the mouth of the Mersey to the north end of the Liverpool and Bootle docks system. Since 1967 the cormorant has enjoyed legal protection, but its great prowess as a catcher of fish – with a swirling grace underwater that belies its awkward, flap-footed gait on land – makes it universally unpopular with anglers.

The recently published and impressively authoritative *Birds Britannica* calls the Great Cormorant (Phalacrocorax carbo) a 'powerfully heraldic bird' with an 'ancient status as a creature of ill omen', possibly due to its habit of holding out its drying wings 'like an openly-draped black cloak'.

It describes adults in breeding plumage as having 'a strong bronze-brown sheen to the back and wings, while the black feathers are variously glossed bottle-green, blue and even purplish in some lights. With their erect crests, bright yellow-orange facial skin, white lozenges on the flanks and frosty throat plumes, they can be remarkably handsome birds'.

Incidentally, the cormorant has no crest, unlike its smaller cousin, the shag – a lucky escape in terms of Liverpool's heraldry, perhaps.

A newer school of thought, however, contends that historically the Liver Bird is neither cormorant nor shoveler nor spoon-bill, but a white-tailed sea eagle – a large, fish-eating species that was a common sight in the Mersey estuary until the early 20th century. Certainly, it has compelling associations with the Eagle & Child armorial device of the Stanleys, Earls of Derby – the regional overlords once based at Knowsley Hall (see p40). Indeed, another eagle, some 700 years old, represents the first time an emblematic bird was found in association with Liverpool – appearing as it does upon the 'common seal' granted to the city following the reign of King John Plantagenet. The earliest surviving impression, from 1352, is in the British Museum, while NML holds four later impressions dating back to 1458.

Although the obscurely-rendered bird (facing to the right, as opposed to the bird on the coat of arms) resembles a dove with an olive branch in its beak, there is strong evidence to suggest otherwise. *The Story of Liverpool,* written by F.A. Bailey and R. Millington and published in 1957 by the Council to commemorate the 750th anniversary of the signing of Liverpool's First Charter by King John, identifies 'a crudely-drawn eagle over a label inscribed Johannis (of John), signifying the emblematic eagle of St John the Divine, and doubtless intended as a flattering compliment to the King; so also were the Plantagenet emblems of the broom-sprig and the crescent with star'.

So, back when it all began, Liverpool had an eagle. It lasted until the town was besieged in 1644 during the English Civil War, when Royalist soldiers loyal to Prince Rupert (grandson of James I) confiscated the seal. In 1655 it was redrawn – by some unknown and apparently amateurish artist – with a 'leaver' instead of an eagle. The original seal turned up almost a century later but was inadvertently destroyed rather than its replacement.

The most recent impression of Liverpool's corporate seal, dating from 1561

Kismet, conjecture, sophistry, subterfuge and folly, then, have all contributed to the creation of the enigmatic beast we now call the Liver Bird. Perhaps this persistent ambiguity explains why, even after the coat of arms was spelled out, representations of the bird refused to conform to type, fusing arbitrary and incompatible features from the eagle, cormorant and duck, to name but three.

Long or short legs, webbed feet or talons, narrow bills or sharp beaks. An ornithological phantom, 'cut and carved in all shapes' as Lancashire historian Matthew Gregson noted in 1817, 'from a goose to a long-necked heron'. The 'lever-bird' that never was but just might – on some Mersey flight of fancy – have been.

ATHENS ON THE MERSEY

'Liverpool, thanks to modern science and commercial enterprise, to the spirit and intelligence of the townsmen, and to the administration of the Mersey Docks and Harbour Board, has become a wonder of the world. It is the New York of Europe, a world-city rather than merely British provincial'.

This breathless salutation appeared in the *Illustrated London News* in 1886. The occasion, an 'International Exhibition of Navigation, Commerce and Industry in Liverpool, England' opened by Queen Victoria on 11 May with a ceremonial key engraved with a Liver Bird, in the same year that the steam-powered underground Mersey Railway was opened.

Six years earlier, Liverpool had been granted city status by the monarch. Its population – well over 500,000 – had almost doubled during the 1850s, mainly due to an influx of Irish immigrants. On average, vessels totalling just under five million tons were paying

Commemorative key presented to Queen Victoria, Liverpool Exhibition 1886

St George's Hall, Liverpool's
neoclassical triumph

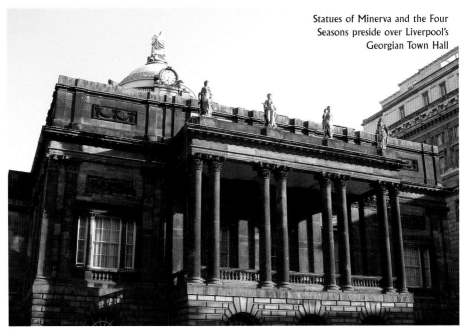

Statues of Minerva and the Four Seasons preside over Liverpool's Georgian Town Hall

dues every year to arguably the largest port on the planet.

The transatlantic slave trade helped to fund this phenomenal growth in the late 18th century, supplanted in time by mercantile shipping and passenger traffic – Liverpool was the departure point for nine million emigrants to America alone from 1821 onwards. Industry and innovation abounded in a port well-connected to the manufacturing heartland of northern England. Vast personal fortunes were amassed and a wealthy middle class sought inspiration from both antiquity and the Renaissance, to beautify their home town during an ongoing building boom – with a distinctive, prestigious motif. The Liver Bird, alone or in the coat of arms, appeared upon everything from cultural institutions and commodity exchanges to lamp standards and local porcelain.

Further carved ornament consisted of nautical imagery, fish, dolphins, mermaids and ships for example, as well as fruit and foliage symbolising abundance, bounty and growth. There were allegorical figures representing commerce, industry and navigation, and Greek and Roman deities such as Poseidon/Neptune (god of the sea), Apollo (for enlightenment and music), Athena/Minerva (wisdom) and Hermes/Mercury (communication and speed).

St George's Hall, completed in 1854, is the ultimate expression of Liverpool's love affair with neoclassicism at the height of British fascination with so-called Greek Revival architecture. As city historian James Picton noted in 1858, 'Everything was to be modelled from the Parthenon'. The building's windows, doors, walls and ceiling teem with Liver Birds, placing this magnificent shrine to the classical world in a precise geographical and historical context.

It was originally designed by Harvey Lonsdale Elmes, but ultimately its creation – particularly the stunning interior – was overseen by Charles Robert Cockerell. An archaeologist and writer, he became president of the Royal Institute of British Architects in 1860 and designed several Bank of England buildings, including the branch on Liverpool's Castle Street.

It was Cockerell's tour of the Mediterranean and Asia Minor from 1809 to 1816, accompanied by Liverpool architect John Foster Junior – who would later design the city's St John's Market and a miniature temple called the Oratory – that kindled the Victorian rediscovery of Greece as the birth-place of western culture and civilisation. Months after Lord Elgin transported the Parthenon's famous friezes from Athens to London, the pair removed similarly significant sculptures from a temple of Apollo at Bassae in central Greece. Fittingly, St George's Hall has replicas of the Elgin Marbles in its south-ern entrance, while the nearby Walker Art Gallery possesses plaster casts from both sets of friezes.

While Cockerill and Foster excavated in Greece, a handful of Liverpool artists studied and copied classical sculpture in Rome under the patronage of rich businessmen back home. John Gibson learned from the mastersculptor Antonio Canova, while John Warrington Wood worked from Italy to produce the figures of Michaelangelo, Raphael and the female personification of Liverpool – complete with faithful Liver Bird – for the exterior and roof of the Walker. In the 1830s B.E. Spence, a student of the Liverpool Academy, almost certainly studied the Bassae casts when they were displayed at the Royal Institution (precursor to the city's first public library) on Colquitt Street.

Such artistic pretensions, allied to its phenomenal mercantile prowess, elevated Liverpool in its own narcissistic eyes above other provincial British towns as a serious rival to the capital. A maritime city state for the modern era, inspired first by ancient Athens, and then Renaissance Venice, Florence and Genoa, altogether grander and more cosmopolitan than its parochial neighbours with their workshop vocations. Could the ubiquitous symbol adorning its buildings be anything other than mythical?

Victorian paintings of Liverpool's waterfront assumed a Venetian air. William Roscoe, the city's esteemed man of letters, urged its mer-chant plutocracy to promote Florentine ideals in culture and learning. In 1895 Philip Henry Rathbone, of the eminent family of Liverpool patricians and politicians, touched upon the subject in a letter to the Corporation's Finance Committee, asking it to complete a series of extravagant friezes along the façade of St George's Hall.

He talked of 'the race of civilisation' and – with an uncanny prescience for 20th centu-ry Liverpool's fate – pondered the demise of Venice. 'At one time, through her position, she became the centre of trade to the East, and employed her wealth in raising a city of glorious palaces. By the discovery of the Cape passage to India she lost that advantage, her trade disappeared, but St Marks and her palaces remained…

'The reason is simple enough: you cannot

Original architect drawing, Royal Liver Building

Carl Bernard Bartels

get a sense of citizenship by any amount of meanly-built and ignoble streets, but you can create a warm and living affection by the erection of noble public buildings, remarkable not only for grandeur but for beauty of decoration, which formulate the nobler and finer feelings and ideas of the citizens, and stand day by day as living witness that the life lived in that city has been one not unworthy of the highest and most developed form of humanity. This is true of architecture as it is of no other form of art or literature...'

At Rathbone's personal expense, the friezes – recounting the story of Liverpool and featuring a Liver Bird in one panel – were eventually finished. One of their executants was Charles J. Allen, one of precious few architectural sculptors in the Victorian era whose names have been recorded for posterity.

Allen worked well into the 20th century, embracing what was termed New Sculpture – a more 'naturalistic' style than the neoclassical work produced by the likes of Gibson, Spence and Warrington-Wood – and witnessing Liverpool's second Greek Revival in which inspiration was drawn as much from America as from Europe, assisted by breakthroughs in construction and engineering using concrete and steel.

By 1901 the city owned one seventh of the world's shipping, with the Mersey registering a third more tonnage (over 10 million) year on year and handling much bigger ships than the more shallow Thames. Six years later, Liverpool celebrated its 700th birthday with an 'Anniversary Festival', featuring a pageant of Liver Birds on poles and a procession of banners, and architect Walter Aubrey Thomas was commissioned to design the skyscraping

Royal Liver Building, with its stupendous copper birds created by German sculptor Carl Bernard Bartels, built at the Pier Head.

Allen was also an inaugural member of the University of Liverpool's School of Architecture and Applied Arts, an influential and avant-garde establishment that regularly sent students across the Pond on work placements.

By virtue of its own maritime history Liverpool already had strong links with the United States and, unlike other British cities, was just as young, modern and imaginative. In 1907 the historian Walter Dixon Scott wrote that it was 'an almost pure product of the 19th century...a city without ancestors'.

The striking colour scheme of today's monumental buildings on the Pier Head and in Liverpool's adjacent business district — a swathe of greyish/creamy white lending them an air of dignity and grandeur — signifies the last major architectural flourish in which the Liver Bird was used as a decorative badge of prestige. It was a deliberate move by local brahmins to create a skyline like the great American cities with which they did business, by adopting both the signature shade of classical architecture and the scale and style of what was called the Beaux Arts — balanced and symmetrical buildings composed of colossal masonry, with columns, balconies and restrained sculpture.

So prominent was this aesthetic genre of architecture in the early 19th century that it even acquired its own name: the Liverpool Manner. Originating in France, the Beaux Arts flourished in America between 1885 and 1920 — ideal for massive buildings like court houses, government offices, museums, hotels and banks in expanding US cities such as Chicago and Philadelphia that sought to plan on a large scale. Bringing what became known as American Commercial Classicism to a city as sophisticated and progressive as Liverpool became a matter of principle and pride.

Liverpool in 1908

There was high-profile dialogue and a 'City Beautiful' conference was staged in 1907. Scholars argued that the colour grey suggested 'solidity of existence' while white and cream signalled 'vivacity'.

By 1930 the Beaux Arts style had all but colonised Liverpool in the throes of a glorious makeover. Charles Reilly, professor of the School of Architecture and Applied Arts, hailed 'a series of great tall simple stone buildings, which in any other age and place would be called palaces, that Liverpool has added to herself' and 'a new outlook on civil architecture in which Liverpool has led the way in this country'. His former pupil Herbert Rowse designed several of them, ranging from Beaux Arts (Martins Bank on Water Street) to futuristic Art Deco (Queensway Tunnel entrances and George's Dock Building), with local sculptors like Herbert Tyson Smith, George T. Capstick and Edmund C. Thompson supplying an appropriately modern strain of Liver Birds — more figurative and often front-facing — to embellish them.

UNGAINLY HYBRIDS AND ROMANTIC SYMBOLS

On 11 January 1932, upon the completion of a landmark building in Liverpool's business district, the *Daily Post & Mercury* made the following observation about the city's symbol: 'The liver seems to be changing since the war. Nearly all our recent designs represent it as a very tranquil creature, a typical example being provided by the three dozen livers surrounding the new Martins Bank headquarters in Water Street, which have not even the customary elevation of the wings associated with the city arms. The Liver

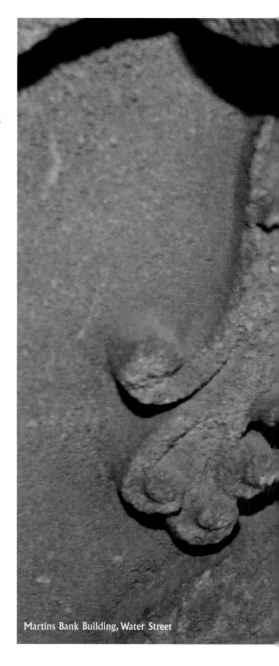

Martins Bank Building, Water Street

Building livers were deliberately designed according to [as the same newspaper reported in 1911] "the traditional type, alert, somewhat fierce in aspect, with half outspread wings".'

But on the bronze doors of the Martins building, as well as the walls and ceiling of its eighth-floor boardroom, the birds were anything but subdued – they were front-facing with raised wings and fabulous plumage. Perhaps less fierce and more defiant after the horrors of the First World War and trauma of the Depression.

The 'tranquil', side-facing birds along the façades of Martins Bank were produced by master sculptor Herbert Tyson Smith. Those at the entrance and upstairs were the work of George T. Capstick and Edmund C. Thompson (the latter, incidentally, also supplied the gilded reliefs of Apollo inside the new Philharmonic Hall, another building designed by Herbert Rowse).

Two years later the same duo were responsible for similarly stylised creatures – front-facing and also gloriously overhead –

upon the Queensway Tunnel entrance and its main ventilation tower, the George's Dock Building at the Pier Head, and later still on the wings of the new Exchange Flags.

These radical geometric designs may have contributed towards the outburst from Robert Gladstone, of no.9 Bluecoat Chambers, in a letter which appeared in the *Post & Mercury* on 27 July 1934. Gladstone, a well-known Liverpool antiquarian and great nephew of the famous statesman, condemned the Liver Bird as 'a modern figment existing only in the disordered imagination of ill-informed and obstinate persons who know nothing about the history of Liverpool and its seal and arms, and don't want to. The real choice lies between a noble eagle [presumably of St John and / or King John Plantagenet] and an offensive cormorant.'

In 1936, upon the discovery of two impressions of the original Liverpool seal that had been lost during the Civil War, he called a special meeting of the local Historic Society in the Royal Institution to denounce the

Queensway Tunnel entrance

cormorant as 'a disgusting, greedy, dirty bird... The arms should be an eagle; they are a cormorant; but the so-called Liver Bird is a monstrosity existing only in the disordered minds of ignorant people.'

Such was the commotion caused by Gladstone and his followers agitating for the eagle's reinstatement that *The Times* weighed in upon the beleaguered Liver Bird's behalf. On 16 April 1936, in a leader-page editorial entitled *The Pool Without the Liver*, it proclaimed: 'The liver is unique. If his mother city disowns him, he will be not even a name... We cannot believe that Liverpool — a great city with a romantic history deserving of a romantic symbol — will submit to such indignity, to say nothing of throwing over an honourable figure now nearly three centuries old.'

The debate continued well into the 1960s with J. Wall, author of *The Quest for the Liver Bird*, maintaining that the birds on the Royal Liver Building were based upon 'an ungainly hybrid creature which bears no resemblance to any known bird, aquatic or otherwise.' As late as the 1990s, the council shelved plans to replace the Liver Bird with the city arms, having deemed the creature 'too aggressive', but backtracked in the face of a *Liverpool Echo*-led campaign.

The purists never got their way, but Liver Bird numbers did decrease in the latter half of the 20th century. With the advent of air travel and containerisation, combined with the slow extinction of northern England's traditional manufacturing heritage, the port economy plunged into rapid decline and decorative sculpture passed out of fashion as a costly extravagance. Liverpool's affluent and

Ceremonial illustration for opening of Queensway Tunnel 1934

often philanthropic merchant class had long since migrated to the suburbs and further afield – a historical phenomenon throughout post-industrial provincial Britain – and like Rome in the Dark Ages, the city centre was left with monuments without meaning.

A working-class exodus followed, too, as Liverpool's population halved over 50 traumatic years. Mass demolition and brutalist redevelopment may have been avoided – with a fabulous legacy of handsome architecture bequeathed in situ – but even the city's current regeneration has occasioned thoughtless and heathen extermination of its mythical symbol.

Those Liver Birds left standing have survived dereliction, vandalism, pollution and a corrosive coastal climate. Fitting, then, that the original bird from the roof of the Walker Art Gallery now roosts inside the Conservation Centre that has pioneered laser cleaning to preserve the city's rich sculptural heritage. Liverpool, reborn and re-invented, is once more recognising the value of the Liver Bird as a historic symbol and world-famous brand. This book, more an enthusiast's almanac than a definitive catalogue, celebrates an endangered species that demands protection and reintroduction into its natural habitat. Explore and enjoy.

Advertising hoarding, Scotland Road

Royal Liver Building and
waterfront from Egremont

FROM THE NML COLLECTION

Between them, National Museums Liverpool and the Town Hall contributed several items featuring Liver Birds that appeared in a 1991 exhibition at the former Liverpool Museum, such as early Victorian earthenware and porcelain, a bandmaster's jacket, life belt and silver snuffer tray, and a mustard pot and toast fork. Other notable NML artifacts include:

A stained-glass memorial (top left) to employees of the Liverpool-based Bibby shipping line, who lost their lives during World War Two. A smoky-grey Liver Bird, with wings lowered, yellow webbed feet, seaweed in bill and the aqualine shape and uptilted head of a cormorant, stands faithfully at the side of a stevedore (whose angular frame has Cubist overtones) on a Liverpool quay, within a border decorated with zodiac signs. Bibby lost two vessels: the *Yorkshire* was torpedoed off the French coast in 1939 with 58 deaths, and the *Shropshire* was attacked off Greenland in 1941 with light casualties. Its head office is now in the former Union Newsroom on Duke Street.

A 3ft-tall stone finial (bottom left) in the shape of a Liver Bird, with a short, conical beak, formerly perched on spires above the old St John's Market designed by John Foster Junior in 1820, rebuilt in 1891 and demolished in 1964. The market, like the Overhead Railway, Customs House, Sailors' Home and original Exchange Flags, is one of Liverpool's lost treasures. As big as St George's Hall, it had 130 arched window bays and a timber roof supported by cast-iron columns. An 1827 watercolour painting of it by Samuel Austin, featuring African faces among the crowds, hangs in the Lady Lever Gallery on the Wirral.

A Mersey Railway Company wooden plaque (top right) showing a buff-coloured Liver Bird with a short, sharp beak and vertical, pointed wings. Its long slender neck, gangling legs and thick shaggy rump are reminiscent of an ostrich. An embroidered picture of the Mersey Railway features the company's logo again and a white, heron-like Liver Bird. Opened on 1 February 1886, this was the world's first true underwater railway and the first to convert from steam to electric (in 1903). On the inaugural day 36,000 passengers used the trains between James Street and Birkenhead's Green Lane.

The regimental colour of the 2nd Royal Liverpool Volunteers (bottom right) with the city arms, featuring two goose-like Liver Birds with black plumage, encircled by a garland of coral roses. The flag dates back to the late 18th century when the Blues, as they were known, saw service in the American War of Independence and West Indies. The senior captain was Banastre Tarleton, born on Water Street, already serving in America and destined to distinguish himself as a cavalry officer. After an expedition against Spanish-controlled Nicaragua and Honduras, the regiment was bolstered by drafts from the Loyal Irish Corps and a few recruits from New York City — where an advertisement in one of the city's newspapers called for 'gentlemen volunteers wishing to serve their king and country on the grand expedition to the Spanish Main, desirous not only of enriching themselves by plundering the gold mines of Mexico, Peru etc, but as gallant heroes in humbling the pride of Spain'. The Blues returned to Liverpool in 1784 whereupon they were disbanded.

FROM THE FIRE BOBBIES

Among the memorabilia at the Merseyside Fire Service Museum in Crosby are brass helmets engraved with Liver Birds from the Liverpool Salvage Corps (the brigade's original name) of the mid-1800s, plus a police helmet with another bird (the fire brigade was initially part of Liverpool City Police Force). Also on display is an authentic Royal Insurance fire mark, again featuring a Liver Bird. In the early 19th century, fire marks were affixed to the exterior of premises to indicate their insurers. If a property was ablaze, only the brigade that

belonged to the relevant insurer would extinguish it. Nearby is a plaque for the now defunct Merseyside County Fire Brigade (formed from the respective brigades of Liverpool, Birkenhead, Bootle, Wallasey and Southport in the early 1970s) with a black Liver Bird draping its wings in true cormorant fashion. Further exhibits include historic fire engines, Victorian ladders and water pumps, and breathing apparatus and bomb detonators from World War Two, when Liverpool firefighters won nine George Crosses.

GOING, GOING...

Highfield Street waterworks, Shaw Street gas sub station, Vernon Street Post Office, Breck Road Barclays Bank. All recorded on a list of locations with Liver Birds for an exhibition at Liverpool Museum in 1991, and all since gone. The Liver Bird count is falling steadily due to longstanding neglect, chronic damage and the city's ongoing redevelopment, with some birds periodically reappearing in property and memorabilia auctions and others, no doubt, finding their way into private collections.

In the foyer of the Liverpool Community College on Clarence Street (between Mount Pleasant and Brownlow Hill) are the legs and tail of a Liver Bird that stood above the inscription 'Literature' over the entrance of a 'pupil teacher school' built in 1897 and demolished in 1999 (it had other birds, too, carved above different academic disciplines).

A pair of webbed feet are all that remain of the Liver Bird which, along with dolphins, supported the cast-iron fountain in Wavertree Park, near to the site of the old Botanic Gardens. Gone, too, are the heads of the birds on the gate piers of Newsham Park, off Prescot Road. The four gates of the Palm House in Sefton Park also featured Liver Birds with lions and eagles, all now missing.

More recently, a sign featuring a duck-like Liver Bird was removed from the Hanover Hotel in the city centre, and a fabulous tiled mural of Liverpool with another bird as its centrepiece was breezily destroyed when the Spiral Staircase public house on Old Hall Street was demolished in 2005 to make way for a new office block.

Liver Birds formerly perched upon lamp standards (probably converted tram poles) along Menlove Avenue in south Liverpool. A letter to the *Post & Mercury*, dated 12 June 1936, noted birds in the shape of mace stands in the Parish Church on the Strand, 'more resembling the so-called liver than any cormorant, and with the mysterious seaweed in their mouths. These are said to date from about 1700.' Wartime bombing probably accounted for them.

Back in the 18th century, one stood on top of the old Town Hall and was (so the story goes) fired upon by rioting sailors who shouted, 'Aim for the goose!' Another, with raised wings, occupied a rainwater spout at St Peter's Church on Church Street, dating from 1711 and demolished in 1922.

In 1931 a free-standing statue of a Liver Bird was erected upon the roof of the *Daily Post's* London offices at Mersey House on Fleet Street (now home to Goldman Sachs). Its whereabouts are unknown, like those of the birds upon the Adelphi Hotel near Gloucester Road tube station and ship's gangway boards in the National Maritime Museum, Greenwich.

THE LIVER BIRDS OF LONDON, MANCHESTER AND ELSEWHERE

At 68 Lombard Street in the City of London are four columns, their capitals featuring three front-facing Liver Birds with raised wings and curled sprigs of seaweed in their bills (left). A grasshopper sits upon a gable outside. The street was named after Italian bankers from Lombardy who settled here in the 13th century, and these buildings are the former London offices of Martins Bank, listed on this site as early as 1794 in *Kent's Directory*. In 1918, Martins was acquired by the Bank of Liverpool but retained its name and boasted 'over 560 offices and agents in all the principal towns at home and abroad' with its headquarters on Water Street. The grasshopper refers to the inn, where Elizabethan banker Thomas Gresham traded.

Due west at Smithfield market (built 1868) is another Liver Bird, this time below a female statue of Liverpool — along with fellow personifications of London, Edinburgh and Dublin that together represent the major towns to which meat was despatched.

Martins were prolific and familiar exporters of the Liver Bird in the early 20th century. A former branch on Claughton's Park Road North on the Wirral (below opposite), for example, features an almost identical bird to those decorating the Water Street HQ, while the Liver Bird and grasshopper from the bank's old Manchester office (below) are still visible at 47 Spring Gardens (now occupied by fashion boutique Vivienne Westwood).

Manchester has another carved Liver Bird on the façade of the former Free Trade Hall on Peter Street (right). It is one of several emblems of Lancashire and Cheshire towns that campaigned against the Corn Laws in the 1840s, when the industrial classes overturned the price of grain set by the land-owning aristocracy to counter cheaper imports.

Liver Birds also appear as part of the Liverpool coat of arms — very much in the Herbert Tyson Smith mould — upon two large stone urns (bottom right) in Portmeirion, the Italianate village built by Clough Williams-Ellis in North Wales from 1925 to 1975.

MASTER AT WORK

'We shall require fifteen modelled fibrous plaster plaques as decorations on the wall of the Newsroom in this new building. The plaques are to represent the twelve signs of the Zodiac (being the outer plaques) with one central plaques showing the Liver Bird, and the two remaining centre plaques to show the Corn Trade Association's device of three wheat-sheaves.'

These lines appear in a letter dated 1955 from the trustees of the Corn Exchange (on Fenwick Street) to mastersculptor George Herbert Tyson Smith, the man responsible for the definitive version of Liverpool's coat of arms. The Corn Exchange was being rebuilt after war damage, but sadly the Liver Bird in question has disappeared.

Much of his work, however, is still visible. Those are his Liver Birds lining the walls of the Martins Bank Building on Water Street. His shells, dolphins and octopuses adorn Spinney House on Church Street, the last major building in Liverpool to incorporate decorative sculpture. And his coat of arms can be found on the Cenotaph (St George's Plateau), Municipal Buildings (Dale Street), Blitz Memorial (Anfield Cemetery) and the entrance to the old fruit market on Prescot Road (Old Swan). The central bird in the shield also stands above the main entrance to Bluecoat Chambers (his former studio) and the upper bird is the template for the trio on the crest that he created for the University of Liverpool.

Born in 1883 and a former student at the School of Architecture and Applied Arts, he set up his own practice in 1912 before serving with the Royal Flying Corps in World War One.

In 1925, as the city of Paris staged a seminal exhibition that glorified Art Deco and the Jazz Age, he moved his studio to Bluecoat Chambers while living at 169 Grove Street (top of Myrtle Street).

The city's Central Library Record Office has over 100 boxes of Smith's personal archives, including correspondence like the Corn Exchange letter, orders and invoices for stone and marble, and architects plans. There are sketches and doodles of Liver Birds, the coat of arms with its comic-book mermen, and assorted sea creatures on tracing paper – 'classical motifs reduced to geometric stylisations' as one scholar puts it. For an Exchange Newsroom Memorial commission, Smith created half a dozen versions of a Liver Bird – one with a letter in its bill.

Smith lived through two world wars and inscribed the names of hundreds of their Liverpudlian victims on memorials. Until his death aged 89 in 1972, he remained the dominant figure in local sculpture.

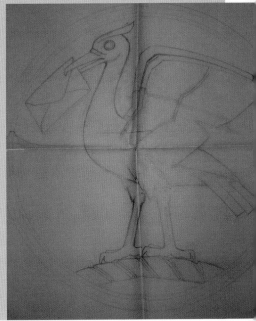

NOT TO BE CONFUSED

Not all of the feathers in Liverpool belong to Liver Birds. The creature on the gates of the Philharmonic Hotel at the corner of Hardman Street and Hope Street is a phoenix rising from the flames (top left), while the bird in the stained-glass window (bottom left) of Stanley House at 151 Dale Street (at the corner with Fontenoy Street) is a dove with an olive branch in its beak. This building originally housed the Liverpool branch of the Blackburn Philanthropic Assurance Company, and the dove is part of the Blackburn coat of arms – featuring three bees, a bugle horn and thread of a shuttle to represent the art of weaving.

A common sight around the wider Liverpool area is the 'eagle and child', the device of the Stanley family, Earls of Derby, landowners in south Lancashire since the late 15th century. The motif appears upon the gates of the 17th Earl of Derby Memorial at Knowsley Hall, the family's traditional seat, and also public houses like the Linacre Hotel in Bootle (almost 30 pubs in the country are actually called The Eagle and Child). Once again it has speculative origins. It may derive from the Greek myth of Ganymede, the handsome Trojan youth carried off by Zeus in the form of an eagle to serve as cupbearer to the gods – the Stanleys being the hereditary cupbearers to the King of England. Alternatively there is the hypothesis of the white-tailed sea eagle, reintroduced to Britain in the 1970s and believed by some to be the basis for the Liver Bird itself. The species has a fabled reputation for baby snatching, and legend has it that a Stanley ancestor deliberately placed his own illegitimate child beneath an eagle's nest in the grounds of his estate to be discovered and fostered by his wife.

Another eagle stands in sculpture at the entrance to the Metropolitan Cathedral and upon a wooden plaque inside Church House, the administrative centre for the Diocese of Liverpool, at the corner of Hanover Street and Duke Street. This is the emblem of St John the Evangelist that appears in the Book of Ezekiel. Again, this being the same symbol of King John Plantagenet who acknowledged St John as his patron saint and whose family granted Liverpool its seal, the eagle could be construed, technically, as a Liver Bird.

CITY CENTRE

1. Port of Liverpool Building, Pier Head
2. George's Dock Building, Pier Head
3. Cunard Building, Pier Head
4. Royal Liver Building, Pier Head
5. The Liverpool, James Street
6. Halifax House, 5 Fenwick Street
7. Nos. 60-62 Castle Street
8. Victoria Chambers, 42 Castle Street
9. Nos. 34-36 Castle Street
10. No. 16 North John Street
11. Nos. 3-5 Castle Street
12. No. 3 Water Street
13. No. 1 Water Street
14. Town Hall, Castle Street
15. Exchange Flags
16. Martins Bank Building, 7 Water Street
17. New Zealand House, Water Street
18. Mersey Chambers, Covent Garden
19. Royal & Sun Alliance, Old Hall Street
20. Cotton Exchange, Old Hall Street
21. Exchange Street Station, Tithebarn Street
22. Sun Alliance House, Tithebarn Street
23. No. 1 Dale Street
24. Union Marine Buildings, 11 Dale Street
25. Ye Hole in Ye Wall, 4-6 Hackins Hey
26. Trident House, 31 Dale Street
27. No. 79 Tithebarn Street
28. City Transport Offices, 24 Hatton Garden
29. Youth Courts, Hatton Garden
30. Queensway Tunnel, Old Haymarket
31. No. 45 Victoria Street
32. Union House, 21 Victoria Street
33. Municipal Buildings, Dale Street
34. Municipal Annexe, 68 Dale Street
35. Education Offices, 14 Sir Thomas Street
36. Conservation Centre, Whitechapel
37. Nos. 16-18 Whitechapel
38. No. 12 Williamson Street
39. Compton House, 33-45 Church Street
40. No. 69 Church Street
41. Bluecoat Chambers, School Lane
42. No. 16 Wood Street
43. Nos. 43-47 Bold Street
44. Former Lloyds Bank, 66-68 Bold Street
45. Britannia Adelphi Hotel, Ranelagh Place
46. Central Hall, Mount Pleasant
47. McHale's Irish American Bar, Lime Street
48. St George's Hall, Lime Street
49. No. 139 Dale Street
50. Cenotaph, St George's Plateau
51. World Museum, William Brown Street
52. Picton Library, William Brown Street
53. Walker Art Gallery, William Brown Street
54. County Sessions House, William Brown St
55. Nos. 34-48 London Road
56. Seymour Chambers, 92-100 London Road
57. Pembroke Place, 106 London Road
58. Royal Infirmary, Pembroke Place
59. Victoria Building, Brownlow Hill
60. University of Liverpool Precinct
61. John Moores University, Mount Pleasant
62. Back Maryland Street
63. Hahnemann Hospital, 42 Hope Street
64. Blackburne Arms, Catharine Street
65. Anglican Cathedral, St James Road

WILLIAM BROWN ST

LONDON RD

PEMBROKE PLACE

JOHN'S LANE

LIME ST

BROWNLOW ST

MOUNT PLEASANT

RENSHAW ST

NELAGH ST

BOLD ST

WOOD ST

FLEET ST

SEEL ST

HARDMAN ST

RODNEY ST

HOPE ST

UPPER DUKE ST

GREAT GEORGE ST

45

1. Port of Liverpool Building, Pier Head

Two beautiful stained-glass windows by G. Wragge & Co of Salford, in a baroque domed palace built for the Mersey Docks & Harbour Board Building in 1907 — the first of the Three Graces on the waterfront.

In the main atrium, an improvised coat of arms for the MD&HB (1) depicts Neptune with trident (standing on waves) and wing-heeled Mercury (on land), flanking a shield containing a white Liver Bird and blue starfish, separated by the River Mersey.

Above the shield is a lighthouse and dolphin surmounted on a knight's helmet. Below the arms is part of the motto of the company, from Psalm 107, which is also engraved in gilt letters around the balcony above the ground floor: 'They that go down to the sea in ships that do business in great waters, these see the works of the Lord and his wonders of the deep.'

Towards the first floor, among the arms of British colonies in stained glass that accompany the curving staircase, is another, greyer Liver Bird (2), wings raised this time and with webbed feet instead of talons, in an ornate circle with 'Liverpool' in a scroll below.

MD&HB had been previously based in the old Customs House at Canning Place, which would be demolished after World War Two. Their new home, designed by Arnold Thornley with Briggs and Wolstenholme (and possibly borrowed from a competition entry for the Anglican Cathedral five years earlier), marked Liverpool's zenith as one of the greatest ports of the Empire, registering £237 million of cargo and more tonnage than London by 1905.

2. George's Dock Building, Pier Head

A colony of very figurative Liver Birds of different shapes, sizes and styles on a Grade II listed Art Deco building, often referred to as the original Fourth Grace. Dating from 1934, the year of Joyce's *Ulysses* and Orwell's *Down And Out In Paris And London*, its monolithic shape was apparently inspired by Howard Carter's excavations in Egypt a decade earlier. There's a touch of Flash Gordon, too, about the futuristic details that compensate for an otherwise stark and simple exterior.

One of six ventilation towers − along with four grand entrances − for the Queensway Tunnel, conceived by Herbert Rowse (the architect behind the Martins Bank, India Buildings and Philharmonic Hall) in sharp contrast to the dominant Victorian gothic and neoclassical landscape of Liverpool, it dazzles when the sun catches its Portland Stone face at the right angle.

Ventilation, though, was only considered halfway through excavation of the tunnel. In 1930, Queensway engineers were alarmed by reports from America that people had been 'gassed' by carbon monoxide (exhaust) fumes in a Pittsburgh land tunnel. An official was despatched to New York to study the much shorter Holland Tunnel, opened three years earlier, that linked Manhattan with New Jersey (similarly relieving ferry congestion) and was equipped with four ventilation towers pumping fresh air under the Hudson River.

Consequently, in 1931 Rowse was commissioned to design Queensway's towers with virtually no architectural precedent, achieving a masterly blend of the utilitarian and aesthetic. A commemorative book

(2)

published in 1934 and entitled *The Story of the Mersey Tunnel Officially Named Queensway*, noted that 'Mr Rowse's buildings follow very closely the shapes dictated by the plant within them'. On the five unmanned towers that complement the George's Dock Building on either side of the Mersey, he dispensed with windows entirely to insulate the noise and vibrations within.

Here, at the base of the north and south elevations, are weathered reliefs of Liver Birds in conventional profile within discs and embellished with horizontal obelisks and striking zig-zag patterns (1). Echoes of their broad, fan-like wings are found on the birds gracing the former façade of Watson Prickard in the city centre (see no. 16 North John Street).

Above the two entrances of the west wall (facing the Port of Liverpool Building) the birds are startlingly different — asymmetric, head-on, mid-flight, like the insignia of some fabulous sci-fi uniform (2). Also, see the overhead variations on the arches of the Queensway Tunnel entrances at Haymarket and Birkenhead.

High up, on each face of the central shaft, they become three-dimensional sculptures (3) nesting on columns either side of fantastical relief panels called 'Ventilation' (see also 'Speed: the Modern Mercury' and the four figures representing Civil Engineering, Construction, Architecture and Decoration). With their large, upraised wings, exotic bills, and fabulous crests and ruffs, they look more like Mesoamerican birds of paradise than the hybrid cormorant that Liverpudlians had come to recognise. There are tiny wooden versions (4) just inside both entrances on the west face, perched above the original revolving doors in owl-like vigilance.

By the 1930s, evidently, there was a departure from traditional representations of Liver Birds, with front-facing sculptures de rigeur.

Edmund C. Thompson and George C. Capstick, the decorative sculptors for the George's Dock Building, had created similarly 'modern' birds for the doors of Martins Bank on Water Street two years earlier (in collaboration with Herbert Tyson Smith). In 1937, they had further refined their designs for the front-facing Liver Birds carved upon the all-new Exchange Flags.

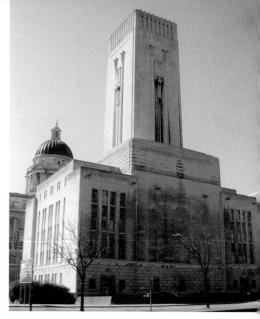

3. Cunard Building, Pier Head

A small, stocky-legged Liver Bird in a simple roundel on the west elevation (facing the Mersey) of this lavishly decorated palazzo – Grade II listed and the last of the Graces, built for the Cunard shipping line between 1914 and 1916.

It is one of a series of carved port crests including London, Bristol, Plymouth, Portsmouth, Falmouth, Southampton, Hull, Newcastle, Aberdeen, Leith, Dundee, Glasgow and Queenstown in Ireland. Also featured are the shields of countries allied to Britain in World War One (France, Russia, Italy, Japan, Belgium, Serbia and Montenegro), plus exquisitely detailed heads of people from Britain's overseas 'Dominions', allegorical figures of Storm and Neptune, Peace, War and Britannia, signs of the zodiac and, on each roof corner, 43-ton American eagles holding Cunard shields. The sculptors were Edward O. Griffith and Charles J. Allen (see St George's Hall), working from Pentelicon marble quarried especially in Greece. The architects were Willink & Thicknesse assisted by Charles Mewes and Arthur Davies, who together designed the Ritz Hotel in London.

A 1916 commemorative guidebook entitled *The New Cunard Building* states that 'much wordy warfare has been waged in the attempt to solve the problem of the identity of the Liver, that alleged mythical bird which in the days of unwritten history had its habitat in the sedge-bound stream meandering through what is now the heart of business Liverpool. It is a pretty legend which thus associates the town with one of its first inhabitants – a feathered one – and suggests the alliance of peace and commerce by placing a laurel spray in its mouth'.

Five years later, Cunard opened a second headquarters at 25 Broadway in New York — the first major edifice built in the city after World War One and still one of Lower Manhattan's most architecturally and historically significant structures. At 22 storeys it towers above its Pier Head cousin, but it shares the same rusticated base (Indiana limestone rather than Portland Stone) of arches crowned with carved keystones and boasts a cavernous Great Hall decorated with murals and reliefs of great maritime explorers, classical nautical scenes, Cunard's shipping routes and the arms of Liverpool and other British ports.

The Line was founded by Samuel Cunard of Halifax, Nova Scotia, and George Burns and David MacIver of Glasgow and Liverpool. Its first ship, the *Britannia*, had sailed from Liverpool to North America on 4 July 1840, and seven years later Cunard had established a direct steam-packet service on a weekly basis between Liverpool and New York.

By the late 19th century it was closely associated with both emigrant and luxury tourist travel and between 1892 and 1900, from its berths in the Huskisson, Canada and Alexandra Docks (all Central Docks), Cunard carried 822,076 passengers over a distance of 5,555,000 miles across the Atlantic and Mediterranean. It merged with White Star in 1934 and ran its last passenger service between Liverpool and New York in 1967.

To this day its distinctive red flag has a crowned lion holding a globe, while its red funnel is intersected by three narrow black bands with a broader black band at the top.

4. Royal Liver Building, Pier Head

There's something not just romantic but thrillingly un-British about this spectacle: two powerfully-built, pastel-green birds with wings aloft (1), three times as tall as a man and perched 300ft above the streets on what was the country's tallest building until the tower blocks of the 1960s. Facing away from each other, looking outwards and in, they are the first sighting of the city from the sea and a familiar mirage through windows, over rooftops and on every Liverpool horizon. They have survived strafing from enemy aircraft during World War Two as well as layers of soot and fierce weather (they were removed in 1931 while the girders at their base were reinforced).

Hard though it is to imagine the city's waterfront without them, less than 100 years ago they existed only in the mind of Carl Bernard Bartels, a German mastercarver who settled in London in 1887 at the age of 21. Twenty-three years later he won the competition to design the birds but was arrested as a German national during World War One, imprisoned on the Isle of Man, and then forcibly repatriated. He eventually returned to Britain and lived here until his death in 1955. Only recently have photographs of Bartels come to light, accompanied by a campaign to erect a plaque in his memory inside the Royal Liver Building.

Made from hammered copper plates, bolted onto a metal framework and further held in place by steel rods fastening their breasts and wing-tips to each dome, the birds were pieced together at the Bromsgrove Guild of Applied Arts (famous also for the gates at Buckingham Palace) where a pit was dug and the workshop roof raised to accommodate them.

They were subsequently dismantled and reassembled in Liverpool as the opulent new home of the Royal Liver Friendly Society, designed by Walter Aubrey Thomas (the architect behind the adjacent Tower Building and Queen Insurance Building on Dale Street), neared completion on the site of the old George's Dock.

On 19 June 1911, the *Liverpool Daily Post* heralded the arrival of 'two ornithological artistic effigies that will prove a source of much attraction to citizens and strangers, cosmopolitan and otherwise. Many have noticed the unfinished and ineffective status of the domes of the towers of the new Liver Building. None more so than Mr Thomas, the architect, but the public did not always realise that this defect was, in fact, a tribute to the architect's genius. What more appropriate terminal could be had for these noble towers than the figure of the fabled Liver of proportional height and stately mien to harmonise with the building?

'Two Liver Birds have therefore been secured, and they will shortly take up their residences. They are of the traditional type, alert, somewhat fierce in aspect, with half-outspread wings, guardians of Liverpool and ready symbolically to defend her premier position among the ports of the world.'

Later that year a general strike, fomented by a transport workers dispute, would bring rioting to the city's streets. But the birds symbolised an era of industry, ingenuity and untold wealth for both Liverpool and the Empire. The *Lusitania* was moored on the Mersey and over 35 million tons of shipping were entering and leaving the river annually. For Britain as a whole, 'invisible' earnings from

banking, shipping, insurance and investments reached £3,780 million by 1913.

Its stacked columns and multi-storeyed rows of arched windows inspired by the skyscrapers of Chicago – a city that had arisen just as rapidly as Liverpool – the Royal Liver was a feat of engineering. Under the guidance of Louis Gustave Mouchel, a Parisian who had developed a new technique of reinforcing concrete with iron bars, builders Nuttal & Co erected a giant frame composed of hundreds of 'ribs' (beams and columns) that carried loads of up to 1,500 tons and held together an 11-floor block occupying over an acre of land (Nuttals, incidentally, would later undertake civil engineering for the Queensway Tunnel). There were 483 steps to the towers

ROYAL LIVER FRIENDLY SOCIETY

TRUSTEES:
LORD STANLEY OF ALDERLEY · DR. G.B. CLARK · J.P. NANNETTI, ESQ., M.P., J.P.

COMMITTEE OF MANAGEMENT:

GEORGE E. FARMER. J.P.	WILLIAM HARROP	JOHN E. OWENS
WILLIAM FIELD	MARK LEWIS	EDWARD SIMPSON
WILLIAM GOLDSMITH	EDMUND MARSH	SAMUEL SKELTON. C.C.

TREASURER: ALFRED WRIGHT   SECRETARY: FRANK H. TAUNTON

THIS STONE WAS LAID BY
LORD STANLEY OF ALDERLEY
ON THE 11TH DAY OF MAY 1908.

W. AUBREY THOMAS. ARCHITECT

and electric lifts that travelled at 400ft per minute. The diameter of the clock face was 25ft, the largest in Britain, and illuminated by a pioneering combination of reflectors, sodium lighting and opalescent glass.

At street level there are stone reliefs of richly plumaged Liver Birds (2) beneath crowns, denoting the company's 'Royal' prefix, and framed by swags of fruit on the porticos above the south and west entrances to the building. The latter, facing the river, is modelled on a famous ancient temple at Baalbek in modern-day Lebanon. Nearby is another bird, weatherworn but still visible (3), on the foundation stone laid by Lord Stanley in 1908.

In the foyer of the western entrance, a beautiful gilded bird is mounted in an

ERECTED BY
THE ROYAL LIVER FRIENDLY SOCIETY
TO THE MEMORY OF ITS EMPLOYEES WHO FELL IN THE
WORLD WAR 1939 – 1945
HEAD OFFICE STAFF
JAMES A. ALEXANDER

extravagant cartouche (4) at the top of a flight of stairs, while a series of bronze tablets – all with small Liver Birds (5) – commemorate the opening ceremony, employees who died during both world wars, and the chimes of the clocktower that were 'installed as a memorial to the members of staff of the Royal Liver Friendly Society who made the supreme sacrifice during the World Wars 1914-18, 1939-45'.

More Liver Birds appear on the building's lift doors (6) – taken from the same cast that local sculptor Herbert Tyson Smith used for his Liverpool coat of arms above the entrance to the Municipal Buildings on Dale Street, the Cenotaph on St George's Plateau and the gilded Liver Bird in a cartouche at Bluecoat Chambers.

5. The Liverpool, James Street

A copy of the crest that appears on the bow of HMS *Liverpool* — featuring a dark-coated Liver Bird within a laurel of rope and crowned with sailing ships — is painted over the doorway of the Liverpool public house on James Street. The name of the pub dates from 1984 (a wine dealers originally stood on the site but was destroyed during World War Two), two years after the seventh HMS *Liverpool*, a Type 42 Sea Dart Destroyer built by Cammel Laird shipbuilders of Birkenhead, was accepted into Royal Navy service.

The very first HMS *Liverpool* was a frigate built in the city in 1741, serving off Spain before she was decommissioned 15 years later and replaced by a second vessel that saw service in the Channel, North Sea (capturing two French privateers), Mediterranean and North Atlantic. The third HMS *Liverpool* was launched in Woolwich in 1814 and took part in an expedition against pirates in the Persian Gulf, while the fourth was the flagship of a squadron that sailed from Plymouth in 1869 and circumnavigated the globe.

The fifth HMS *Liverpool*, a 4,800 ton cruiser, was the first to be built of steel (in Barrow) and saw action during World War One when rescuing HMS *Audacious* after that ship had been mined. The penultimate vessel to bear the name was completed in 1938. During World War Two she captured 21 German officers and men on board a Japanese liner, engaged Italian destroyers off Greece, patrolled the Allied Arctic and Malta convoys, and was torpedoed on two separate occasions. She was finally broken up in 1958.

(2)

(3)

(4)

6. Halifax House, 5 Fenwick Street

Two excitable Liver Birds stand facing each other, their wings raised and bills binding together a bundle of rods to form a 'fasces' – the symbols of authority once carried by Roman magistrates and appropriated by Italy's dictatorship in the 1930s – set above a scroll containing the inscription Vis Unita Fortior (Together We Are Stronger).

This striking relief appears several times (1, 2, 3 and 4) on the original head office of the Liverpool Union Bank. In one panel the birds are surrounded by olives, symbolising peace, and in another by Scottish thistles, Lancastrian roses and an Irish shamrock, denoting unity. The Latin inscription was the bank's motto, and its name is also inlaid around a garland containing another Liver Bird on the south façade opposite the India Building (1). Similar reliefs are found on former branch offices of the bank on Bold Street and London Road.

The Liverpool Union Bank was founded in 1835 by coffee dealer Ben Allport, merchants Thomas Firth and John Miller, and steam-packet agent Joseph Pim-Robinson. It was absorbed by Lloyds in 1900, much to the dismay of the local banking community who complained that 'Lancastrian businessmen should be able to undertake the most delicate negotiations with Lancastrian bankers.' After a spell as a branch of the Halifax Building Society, the building now lies unoccupied but was briefly recreated as an antiques shop in 2003 for the remake of the movie Alfie.

7. Nos. 60-62 Castle Street

A colony of Liver Birds adorn this elegant sandstone stack at the corner of Liverpool's traditional business thoroughfare, most recently a hotel bar popular with the judicial community (hence its name Trials) but historically the premises of several banking institutions.

In spandrels, embellished by acanthus or decorative foliage, above the arched entrance is a relief of a Liver Bird (1) and the City of London's heraldic cross of St George. The bird-and-cross motif is repeated over the doors in the vestibule (2), flanked by bearded figures in classical robes, reclining on a chest and pitcher. High up, pairs of carved birds are perched atop Corinthian capitals on the south, east and west elevations (3), and on the ceiling inside the old banking hall is an exquisitely rendered, black enamel Liver Bird (4) in a cartouche (scroll-like ornamental tablet) with fabulous unicorns worked in plaster either side.

The five-storey building was erected in 1868 for the Alliance Bank of Liverpool and the City of London, established six years earlier with directors in both cities. The architects were Lucy & Littler, who had earlier designed the entrances to Anfield Cemetery. In 1871 the Alliance was acquired by the National Bank of Liverpool, which temporarily occupied the building while its own offices were being constructed on nearby Cook Street.

Two years later, it became the headquarters of the North & South Wales Bank, founded earlier in the century (and later to merge with Midland Bank) to cater for rural businessmen and Liverpool's 40,000-plus Welsh population,

many of whom lived in an area around Pall Mall known as Little Wales. At the time, more people in Liverpool spoke Welsh than in Cardiff, Swansea or Wrexham. Among their many places of worship was a cathedral-like Presbyterian Church on Princes Road, and they had their own schools, festivals (see Town Hall), newspaper and special Welsh penny minted as far back as 1788. The famous community in Patagonia came from a clipper, called *Mimosa*, that left Liverpool in 1865.

The bank's capital helped to build row upon row of terraced housing — there are streets in today's Toxteth called Geraint, Enid, Merlin, Modred, Elwy, Voelas, Rhiwlas, Gwydir and Pengwern, and in Vauxhall to the north Menai, Snowdon, Barmouth, Cemaes and Newport, all laid by Welshmen.

Historical footnote: 30ft below the building's ground level are the remains of the dungeons of Liverpool Castle.

8. Victoria Chambers, 42 Castle Street

Before locating its Liver Birds, take a moment to stand on the opposite side of Castle Street and look at the grand scheme of this five-storey, wedding-cake building — recently licked with white paint — then trace the decorative detail at each level. Truly a work of art.

The architects were George Enoch Grayson and Edward Ould, a prolific partnership in the late Victorian period who designed several Renaissance-style premises for banks and businesses in the city — see nos. 3-5 and 34-36 Castle Street as well as Mersey Chambers and the former Bank of Liverpool on Victoria Street. Among their other achievements: shops and housing for Lord Leverhulme's Port Sunlight Village, college buildings for Cambridge University and Turkish baths for several country piles.

Here, at neck-craning height, four sinewy mermen with swirling fish tails blow conch shells from the upper gables, their free hands resting on carved roses. Beneath those mermen at the extreme left and right stand robust and seemingly flightless twin Liver Birds (1) minus

seaweed and facing inwards. Along the same
frieze are more flowers, crests and another pair
of reclining mermen, one facing the street and
the other with his muscular back turned.
The corresponding frieze between the third
and fourth floors, surmounted at each end by
beautiful wrought-iron balconies, features
sharp-beaked griffons and two pairs of cherubs
flanking Liver Birds with raised wings (2).
In the pediment crowning the building,
incidentally, is a heraldic ensemble of dogs,
feathers, shield and crown that represent the
arms of the West Derby Hundred within the
historic county of Lancaster (for a full
interpretation, see the entry for the former
Police Station on Old Swan's Derby Lane).

The date of the building's completion,
1893, is inscribed upon the centre of the
façade (the previous year the honorary
freedom of the city had been conferred upon
William Gladstone, the Liverpool-born Prime
Minister). Over the years it housed offices
for ship owners and brokers, solicitors and
accountants, and the London & Provincial
Bank (latterly National & Provincial).

9. Nos. 34-36 Castle Street

Plenty of feathers amid a tumult of decoration on another financial building designed by Grayson & Ould, this time for the Leyland & Bullins Bank in 1895.

On the east (Castle Street) façade, a pair of Liver Birds dance to the crashing cymbals and blaring horns of two putti or cherubs (1). Nearby another bird, head bowed and sprig in beak, flutters its broad wings next to a bowl filled with fruit (2). High up on the south elevation (Brunswick Street) is a Liver Bird in a coat of arms (but no room on the long, rectangular frieze for a second bird above the crest) with mermen flanked by sleek sailing ships (3).

No wonder the sculptures are so exultant. Thomas Leyland, founder of the eponymously-named bank and three times city mayor, was a man of remarkable fortune. In 1776, while trading with Ireland in humble cereal produce, he won £20,000 in the State Lottery — then, as now, used to replenish government coffers

– and the following year he married his former employer's daughter, inheriting a third of her estate when she died. He invested his wealth in two privateers, the *Lottery* and *Enterprise*, that imported olive oil from Spain and exported African slaves to the New World. Records show that *Enterprise* made £24,430 from one voyage that delivered 412 slaves to Havana in 1802.

That same year, Leyland became a partner in the banking firm of Clarkes & Roscoe – the latter, ironically, being noted slavery abolitionist William Roscoe. Four years later Leyland left to establish his own bank with nephew Richard Bullin on what was then King Street, near Duke Street. In 1827 he died childless, aged 75, leaving the vast sum of £600,000 (estimated at £6 million in 1967). Towards the end of the century the surviving business moved to their new head office in Castle Street and amalgamated in quick succesion with the North & South Wales Bank and Midland Bank. The building is currently occupied by the Royal Bank of Scotland.

10. No. 16 North John Street

Genial Liver Birds, in profile and above the initials WP, appear on two company logos engraved into the marble façade at street level (1) and high up over the junction of North John Street and Cook Street (2). They recall the former headquarters of men's outfitters Watson Prickard, a business that traces its roots back to 1867 when a Mrs Butcher advertised for a 'married manager' to run her hosiery shop on Dale Street.

She gave the job to a bachelor called Watson Prickard, whom she later married. The firm moved to North John Street in 1893, expanding to include specialist departments (notably school uniforms), fitting rooms and a hair salon, and earning a reputation for its personal sevice and integrity.

On the occasion of its centenary in 1967, the company celebrated by unveiling plans for a new building twice the size of the existing store, and a subsequent issue of the *Illustrated Liverpool News* looked ahead to the next 100 years: 'Great grandfathers will be bringing as yet unborn generations into the shop for their school uniforms and it is not inconceivable that the travel department will be stocking special luggage for astronauts.' Sadly, the store closed in the 1990s and has most recently housed a salsa bar-restaurant.

11. Nos. 3-5 Castle Street

Another office designed by Grayson and Ould, this time in red granite for the British & Foreign Marine Insurance Company in 1889. A colourful mosaic frieze over the first floor contains the company's name spelt out on red streamers between two banners — on the left featuring a squat, sooty-black Liver Bird holding a great frond of seaweed, and on the right the cross of St George — further flanked by shipping scenes old and new.

The building's frieze was created by the firm of Antonio Salviati, who died a year after its completion. From his 'laboratory of mosaic art' in Venice, he had revived this ancient craft and made it fashionable among Victorians. His most famous works are: the mosaic restorations in St Mark's Basilica in Venice, those on the Albert Memorial in Hyde Park and Westminster Abbey's high altar screen, a portrait of Abraham Lincoln presented as a gift to the United States, and a massive mural at Stanford University in California (painstakingly recreated after the 1906 San Francisco earthquake). Mosaics can still be seen along the second-floor level of his old shop on London's Regent Street.

Formed in 1863, British & Foreign was one of half-a-dozen Liverpool-based companies established in quick succession that would dominate the world's marine insurance industry from a port which handled 50 percent of all UK exports. The catalyst was the American Civil War: as the demand for raw materials and manufactured goods increased, London insurers began to charge higher premiums at the last minute. In response, Liverpool merchants banded together to provide their own cover. At the time, both ports were regularly exceeding three million in annual tonnage.

Within a year of its formation, British & Foreign was underwriting in Bombay, Calcutta, Madras, Singapore, Honolulu, Montreal, Victoria, Cape of Good Hope, Valparaiso, Melbourne, Hong Kong, Shanghai, Gibraltar and Smyrna. When it was eventually absorbed by Royal Insurance, it had greater reserves than any other marine insurance company in the world.

12. No. 3 Water Street

Adjacent to the golden bird at no. 1 Water Street is this reminder of a rare collaboration between geographically close but charismatically distant cities. In twin arched recesses above the doorway sit not just the arms of Liverpool, but those of Manchester. Between them is a miniature pilaster decorated with a sovereign coin featuring a young Queen Victoria's head in profile, the words Victoria Dei Gratia (Victoria by the grace of God) and the date 1882.

Underneath, an arabesque monogram of the initials M, L, D and B identifies this as a former branch of the Manchester & Liverpool District Bank, formed in 1829 as one of the earliest joint-stock banks in the country (see no. 45 Victoria Street). It issued its own notes (collector's items today) for a short period and had over 50 branches nationwide – each with its own local board of directors – by the 1880s. More commonly known as the District Bank, it was acquired by National Provincial Bank in 1962 and eight years later became part of National Westminster.

13. No. 1 Water Street

Above the entrance to the old offices of the Liverpool Building Society (since acquired by Birmingham Midshires) stands this three-dimensional sculpture — an unusually right-facing and undeniably eye-catching Liver Bird, more conspicous after a recent lick of gold paint. Its S-shaped neck is as long as its drumstick legs, and the plumes of its mechanical wings and tail resemble basaltic columns. The powerful body, hooked beak and emphatically upright, almost human stance suggests some prehistoric flightless bird or incredible roc of eastern legend. The same bird can be found on a larger scale upon Vermont House in Bootle.

14. Town Hall, Castle Street

No Liver Birds, surprisingly, stand on the site of the exterior of the third Town Hall. Dating from 1748, it was almost completely gutted by fire in 1795 and rebuilt under the supervision of London architect James Wyatt, and was a miraculous survivor of the 1941 Blitz.

Instead, a panoply of exotic animals (elephants, camels etc) adorn friezes around the building with Minerva, Roman goddess of wisdom, presiding over the city from the dome above. At the rear, looking onto Exchange Flags, are statues of the Four Seasons which came from the Irish Houses of Parliament. At the front, Queen Victoria, Mark Twain, the Beatles and the city's football teams have all graced the balcony facing Castle Street.

Inside, though, the birds are many and varied. The vestibule has a colourful, encaustic (burned-in) tiled floor of 1848 with Liver Birds in a coat of arms (1) at its centre, as a matching pair in luxuriant foliage (2) in all four corners and striding forward, alone in a simple medallion (3) on all four borders.

N · 1789 - 92 · AND · WAS

Above both the vestibule entrance and the arched doorway leading to the staircase are handsome gold Liver Birds in wooden cartouches (4) while a crestless, gilded bird (5) with the rounded head and short, thin bill of a woodpecker, appears along the drum base of the building's stunning blue-and-gold dome.

In a corridor outside the mayor's office are two hefty cast-iron state braziers in the shape of Liver Birds with quaintly reptilian heads (6). Around the perimeter of the nearby council chambers are two-dozen chairs all with carved Liver Birds (7), all subtly different from one another.

Among the treasures in the ground-floor display cases either side of the staircase: shields and swords of state, bailiff's maces and footman's staves, candelabra and caskets, ewers and vases, flagons and tankards, dessert and fruit bowls, ink stands and snuff boxes. Also behind glass, ceremonial Liver Bird maceholders (8) and a tiny, exquisitely-worked pewter bird (9) mounted on a trophy and presented to the city by Royal Liver Assurance to mark the company's 150th

birthday. Much of the silver dates from the late 18th and early 19th centuries.

Another display cabinet on the staircase landing contains a 12in crystal Liver Bird (10) mounted on a wooden plinth, this time honouring the 150th anniversary of Royal Insurance, founded in 1850. Opposite on the landing is the official mayoral regalia, including a sleeveless chasuble or robe with twin, radiant Liver Birds stitched in gold, green and blue thread (11) upon the chest.

Upstairs, in the moulded cornices of the first-floor ballroom are two more splendid coat of arms (12) with riots of dark-green seaweed enveloping the birds and mermen (note the wonderfully scaly texture of the triton's silver fish tail), both opposite similarly-presented royal arms.

Back in the vestibule, either side of the fireplace, a couple of Bardic Chairs with carved Liver Birds (13 and 14) commemorate two of the four Eisteddfodau (festivals celebrating Welsh music, poetry and literature) held on Merseyside in the early 20th century. They were donated by Lewis's, the department store on Renshaw Street, which staged its own Eisteddfodau for Liverpool's large Welsh population up until the 1950s.

The chair to the right of the fireplace dates from 1884 and is inscribed with Ich Dien (I Serve, from the Prince of Wales motto), Iesu Na'd Gamwaith (Jesus, Suffer Not Iniquity, the motto of Gwynedd or North Wales) and Tywysogaeth Cymru (Principality of Wales). The chair to the left, from 1900, has the words Y Gwir Yn Erbyn Y Byd (Truth Against The World, the festival's slogan and an ancient Bardic recital) and Eisteddfod Genedlaethol Cymru (National Eisteddfod of Wales).

Not here but part of modern Welsh folklore is the Bardic Chair from the 1917 Eisteddfod held over the river in Birkenhead. It was awarded to Hedd Wyn for his poem *The Hero*, written in a Litherland barracks after he had enlisted in the 18th Battalion, Royal Welsh Fusiliers.

When his pseudonym Fleur-de-lis was called out at the festival, it was announced that he had been killed in action in Flanders. The chair became known as Cadair Ddu Birkenhead, the Black Chair of Birkenhead, and was sent to his parents at their remote Merionethshire farmhouse.

15. Exchange Flags

You have to look up high to spot these elegant Liver Birds, two sets of three carved into shallow recesses on the tower elevations of Horton and Walker House (named after local gentry), perched on a stylised River Mersey and peering down on this historic square and its Nelson Monument behind the Town Hall.

Prior to the opening of the Cotton Exchange on Old Hall Street in 1906, for a century this is where business was conducted between cotton merchants and brokers. The old, cloistered buildings were demolished in 1937 to make way for a new, comparatively drab-looking edifice designed by Gunton & Gunton. Construction was interrupted by the war and not completed until 1955.

In superb condition, the birds are the work of Edmund C. Thompson and George C. Capstick, who had previously sculpted the exotic, front-facing Liver Birds for the bronze doorways of the Martins Bank Building and the George's Dock Building's central shaft. Here, they have blended elements from both: the same crest and bill are streamlined, and the feathers of the elevated wings finished with concentric tips, to create a sleeker and still more majestic creature.

(2)

(3)

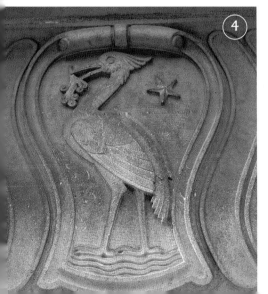

(4)

16. Martins Bank Building, Water Street

Double figures easily for the head count of Liver Birds on, around and inside this Grade II listed, landmark Liverpool building erected in 1932 and now occupied by Barclays Bank. Under the stewardship of chief architect Herbert Rowse, the decorative sculpture was a collaboration between Herbert Tyson Smith (who had previously supplied the coat of arms and relief panels for the Cenotaph on St George's Plateau) and Edmund C. Thompson and George C. Capstick (later to provide the extravagantly-plumaged birds on the George's Dock Building and new Exchange Flags).

Nine years earlier Rowse had designed the monumental, marble-faced India Building on the other side of Water Street. Yet to exercise his plans for the Queensway Tunnel entrances and ventilation towers, or his radical vision for the Philharmonic Hall on Hope Street, this was his second great realisation of American commercial architecture in Liverpool and indeed the UK.

By the early 1930s, the city was not only revelling in its commercial might but increasingly receptive to new ideas in industry

and engineering. As the only major bank based outside London (having merged with the long-established Bank of Liverpool in 1918 and procured 700 branches nationwide) Martins was seeking a new head office, as much as a statement of confidence as practical requirement, and Rowse was the obvious candidate for architect.

A graduate of the Liverpool School of Architecture – at that time dominated by the charismatic Professor Charles Reilly – he had won a scholarship to travel to the United States before returning home to implement what he had seen. Accordingly, although designed on classical Roman lines, the 150ft high Martins Bank boasted a steel-frame construction and advanced system of servicing (ducted pipes and wires, heated ceiling etc).

Such a significant building, faced in Portland stone (stored and cut at the William Moss masonry in Liverpool), demanded the very best sculptural decoration. Based on their work elsewhere, it is not too fanciful to assume that among Thompson and Capstick's contributions were the three Liver Birds intersecting the 9ft by 2ft bronze doorways on Water Street (1). These are arguably prototypes for the birds that would appear on Exchange Flags five years later: the same front-facing aspect, raised wings and straight bills, but fatter breasts and spindlier, bamboo-ringed legs. Above them are women in Norse helmets holding either longboats or printing presses, and on the adjoining walls bald-headed Neptunes with dolphins and African boys holding coins, anchors and ropes.

Over the fifth-floor windows of the front elevation, again in brilliant-white Portland stone, is a shield containing a Liver Bird in profile (2), wings tucked down, surmounting wavy lines representing the River Mersey, and supported by a horizontal triton and mermaid with splendid fish tails, fin-like girdles and Assyrian hairstyles. Above the shield is a grasshopper — a reference to the name of the tavern on London's Lombard Street where moneylender Sir Thomas Gresham practised the country's first banking system in the late 16th century.

The Liver Bird, grasshopper and Mersey motif is repeated in discs (3) either side of the arched main entrance, and there are similar birds in cartouches beneath each of the 30 ground-floor windows (4). Their countenance suggests the hand of Tyson Smith — even the sprig of seaweed in their bills has the same shape and composition as that in his coat of arms outside the Municipal Buildings on Dale Street and Cenotaph on St George's Plateau. Inside, it seems that they saved the best till last. The ceiling of the Jazz Age banking hall (still in use) is embellished with four slate-coloured Liver Birds in gold shields (5), topped with gold grasshoppers, and flanked by serene and voluptuous mermaids with cascades of golden hair.

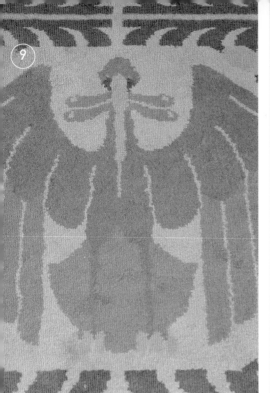

Eight floors up, another artistic tour de force. Drawing the great velvet curtains of the boardroom is like illuminating the ocean floor: the walnut ceiling is awash with mermaids, ships, dolphins, shells, starfish and two types of strutting, long-billed Liver Bird (6 and 7) picked out in gold, emerald green and Indian red. More fabulous birds with huge, angular, bat-like wings, stand with pairs of seahorses either side of the marble chimney pieces (8) and inside the arched window bays. They even reappear in maroon brown and bottle green upon the specially-woven carpet (9), and as an opposing pair upon an elegant mantlepiece in an adjoining room (10). Full frontal and in profile, together they are a reconciliation of the idiosyncratic styles of Smith, Thompson and Capstick.

17. New Zealand House, Water Street

The former premises of the city's New Zealand consulate, designed by Walter Aubrey Thomas in 1893 (almost 30 years before he worked on the Royal Liver Building) and since converted into a night club and restaurant, contains a real rarity – a series of Liver Birds depicted in mid-flight and facing right.

A recent addition to the venue, they are etched as reliefs upon metal panels running behind (1) and below (2) the long bar. With crests resembling ears, elliptic concave cat's eyes, trailing legs and tails, and seemingly hirsute bodies, they are a curious hybrid of marsupial and antipodean seabird – although the seaweed in their beaks signifies a more familiar genus. Intriguing, too, are the accompanying decorative waves on the panels below the bar – artwork with a distinctly oriental feel.

Water Street is one of Liverpool's seven ancient streets, and New Zealand House is a late Victorian addition to a graceful thoroughfare that was once home to brewers, woodcarvers, shoemakers and silversmiths, before welcoming huge office blocks that housed shipping lines, banks and other financial institutions. Its grand but gentle incline begins at the Town Hall and ends at the waterfront – crossing the Strand and continuing down to the Pier Head, lined by the cliff-face facades of the Royal Liver and Cunard Buildings.

18. Mersey Chambers, Covent Garden

The 'Third Liver Bird', as it is commonly known, faces the Royal Liver Building across the Strand from its perch above a carved sailing ship on the building's central bay, its ivory plumage in sharp contrast to the verdigris or rusty green copper feathers of its more famous cousins. Note, too, the mythical stone beasties gnawing away at other less fortunate creatures lower down between the projecting oriel windows.

The Grade II listed Mersey Chambers was designed by George Enoch Grayson, one half of the prolific late-Victorian architectural team, for the T&J Harrison shipping line in 1870. The adjacent grounds of the Parish Church of St Nicholas, itself dating way back to 1327, were laid out as a public garden 20 years later in memory of James Harrison. Founded in 1830, the line possessed over 30 steamers and provided services to the United States, Mexico, West Indies, Brazil, South Africa, India and East Indies.

19. Royal & Sun Alliance, Old Hall Street

On the wall of the Royal's reception (through the main entrance of the massive City Exchange building and up the escalators) is the company's coat of arms: a fire-breathing silver dragon and glossy-black Liver Bird, wings raised with a cormorant's white face and green sprig in its bill (1), together their claws and webbed feet steadying a shield beneath a globe in a crown. They stand upon the motto Tutum Te Sistam, meaning 'We hold you safe' and taken from Virgil's account of the great fire at Troy in the Aeneid. On the opposite wall, a certificate with Liverpool's own heraldry (2) commemorates the company's award of the freedom of the city in 1996 In 'acknowledgement and appreciation of the significant and lifelong contribution made to the commercial life of the City of Liverpool by Royal Insurance plc'.

Not on view but kept in the boardroom are three beautiful Liver Bird stone finials (3), each 3ft high and possibly from the Royal's original head office on the corner of Dale Street and North John Street, opened in 1849, which was known to have sculpture above its main entrance. This building was demolished and rebuilt 50 years later as a gold-domed Liverpool landmark which stands to this day. Consecutively, their wings are lowered, half elevated and fully raised, and all hold seaweed in their short, thick bills.

The Royal was formed because London's insurers refused to cover the fire hazard that was Liverpool's dockside in the early 19th century. In 1802 an inferno destroyed 17 warehouses on the old Goree Piazza with a total loss of £323,000 (around £30 million today), and the Formby Street Fire of 1842 reduced six acres near Great Howard Street to ashes. A circular was issued among the capital's insurance companies stating 'The second town in the Empire has now remained

CITY OF LIVERPOOL

for the greater part of half a century without any public organised means for stopping a fire, or even furnishing sufficient water for the supply of such engines as accident or private interests have occasionally supplied to the town.'

On 11 March 1845 a group of Liverpool businessmen responded by forming a Joint Stock Fire and Life Insurance Association, which became known simply as the Royal. On its first board of directors was cotton planter Josias Booker, dock chairman Charles Turner and J. Bramley-Moore, director of two railway companies and chairman of the Bank of Egypt. A second office was opened in London, and by 1860 the Royal had agents in the US and Canada, South America, the West Indies, Australia, South Africa, India, Russia and Hong Kong. Above the doorway to the Royal Insurance Company building in New York, opened in 1927 at the corner of William Street and Fulton Street in Lower Manhattan, a Liver Bird in relief still accompanies the monogram RIC above the doorway.

By the end of the 19th century the Royal was one of several major companies with headquarters in Liverpool, among them shipping lines Holt, Brocklebank, Cunard and Harrison, shipbuilders Lairds, sugar refiners Tate, soap manufacturers Levers and Bibby, glassmakers Pilkingtons, and bankers Glyn's and Martins.

Despite paying out $7 million after the 1906 San Francisco earthquake, the Royal continued to prosper and in time absorbed other insurers like British & Foreign Marine, Liverpool & London & Globe, and Queen and Sun Alliance.

20. Cotton Exchange, Old Hall Street

A large blue flag in the boardroom of this historic Liverpool institution features a Liver Bird silhouetted in white within a shield above a sprig of the cotton plant (gossypium herbaceum).

The building's ornate Edwardian façade may have gone – demolished in 1967 in what some architectural commentators have described as an act of vandalism – but it remains the headquarters of the Liverpool Cotton Association, opened in 1906 by the Prince and Princess of Wales (their signatures are on the opening page of the priceless visitor's book).

Back then, five million bales of raw cotton were imported to Liverpool every year, and today over 60 percent of the world's cotton is still traded under LCA rules. The first recorded shipment into the port was 26 June 1757, when 28 bags of cotton weighing 150lbs each arrived from Jamaica and were most probably bought and sold in Exchange Flags behind the Town Hall.

At pavement level outside the building is a colossal, allegorical statue of the River Mersey, clasping an anchor, tiller and rope and pouring water over a dolphin, and in the courtyard are two statues of Navigation and Commerce, the only survivors of eight that once stood high up on the roof.

21. Exchange Street Station, Tithebarn Street

It is formerly the western terminus of the Lancashire & Yorkshire Railway and is accordingly decorated with miniature coats of arms of Liverpool (1), Bradford and Manchester in roundels resting on chains held by cherubs. Also on the main façade: a Liver Bird in foliage high on a pediment (2), the signs of the zodiac, and busts of King Edward VII and Queen Alexandra, both of whom attended the official opening of a new terminus here in 1882 when surveyor Thomas Shelmerdine (who designed the City Transport Offices on Hatton Garden and Everton Library) elevated the tracks to accommodate the Leeds & Liverpool Canal.

Handling over 500 daily arrivals and departures at its peak, the station also housed the Exchange Street Hotel, a favourite stop over of World War One poet Siegfried Sassoon. It was closed in 1977 to make way for the new Mersey Rail system, but the classical stone façade — running all the way from Bixteth Street to Pall Mall — was preserved and now fronts an office block called Mercury Court.

22. Sun Alliance House, Tithebarn Street

In an impressive Portland stone relief above the entrance of these former Royal & Sun Alliance premises built in the 1950s, two powerful Liver Birds with curved bills open (see the tongues!) and broad wings aloft, face each other from opposite banks of the River Mersey, over which is a fiery sun incorporating a castle on a rock.

The sun represents the insurance company of the same name, established in the capital in 1710 and now the oldest firm of its kind in existence still trading under its original title. It prospered by acquiring the Westminster Fire Office, Phoenix and London (insurance firms) while developing its business interests first in mainland Europe, and then the US and Canadian markets, South America, Australia, Africa, India and China. The castle, a symbol of strength and security, stands for the Alliance Assurance Company with whom the Sun merged in 1959 before amalgamating with Royal Insurance in 1996.

23. No. 1 Dale Street

A small Liver Bird in one shield, the cross of St George in another, and both affixed to a planet. This is the centrepiece of a sculpture in the tympanum (triangular space over the entrance) of the former head office of the Liverpool & London & Globe Insurance Company, adjacent to the Town Hall and now housing the Royal Bank of Scotland. Supporting the globe are muscular mermaids with long ears and twin tails.

This imposing, Grade II listed building was designed in 1856 by Charles Robert Cockerell, five years after he had replaced the late Harvey Lonsdale Elmes as chief architect for St George's Hall. The carvings were undertaken by Edwin Stirling, assisted by Cockerell's favourite sculptor W.G. Nicholl, who had produced the four sentinal lions on St George's Plateau. Cockerell was a true pioneer of Greek Revival architecture in the early 19th century, travelling to Athens and beyond as an adventurer and archaeologist, and returning to implement classical forms and technology in British towns and cities. He designed several Bank of England buildings in the provinces, including a grand edifice on Castle Street.

The Liverpool & London & Globe was established in 1836 by shipowner George Holt, one of the founders of the Bank of Liverpool (see Sir Thomas Hotel), with a London office opposite the Bank of England at no. 1 Cornhill. Among its first directors were esteemed Liverpool names like Booth, Brocklebank, Hornby, Ewart, Heyworth and Melly. It merged with Royal Insurance in 1919, exactly one year after the end of World War One.

24. Union Marine Buildings, 11 Dale Street

Three diminutive Liver Birds, in profile but subtly different from each other in sculptural detail, appear in roundels above the first storey of this building – two facing each other on Dale Street and the other on the east elevation along Hackins Hey.

Originally the offices of the Queen Insurance Company, the building dates from 1859 and is one of several in Liverpool designed by James Picton – his portfolio includes no. 48 Castle Street, the Fowler's Building on Victoria Street, Hargreaves Building on Chapel Street (now home to the Racquet Club), Brougham Terrace on West Derby Road, and the epic Harthill entrance to Calderstones Park. Central Library's Reading Room on William Brown Street was named after this prolific architect and historian, who was inspired by the glorious façades of Venetian palaces and knighted for his services to the city.

Union Marine, one of a handful of insurance companies formed during the American Civil War (see British & Foreign Marine, 3-5 Castle Street) moved into the building in 1905 and it was renamed in their honour.

25. Ye Hole In Ye Wall, 4-6 Hackins Hey

Beaten upon the magnificent brass canopy above the fireplace in this old watering hole off Dale Street is a slender-necked, open-winged Liver Bird, holding a meticulously-designed sprig of seaweed in its short bill. Higher still is a panel inlaid with griffons, bowls of fruit and two less classifiable birds (shorter necks, longer bills, no seaweed) and engraved with the date 1726 in Roman numerals.

A 'hey' was originally an area of land enclosed by hedges, and the thoroughfare was named after John Hacking, who owned a house, barn and croft on this site in the mid-17th century. The age of the public house is less certain. The current building is thought to date from around 1850 when it was a licensed premises on the ground floor of a warehouse – hence its famous claim to have been the only Liverpool pub with beer drawn from a cellar upstairs. Before then, the site was occupied by a Quaker Meeting House with a burial ground underneath. Breweries, however, are known to have existed on Hackins Hey in the 1750s, so the date above the fireplace may recall the pub's original incarnation somewhere very close to its current home.

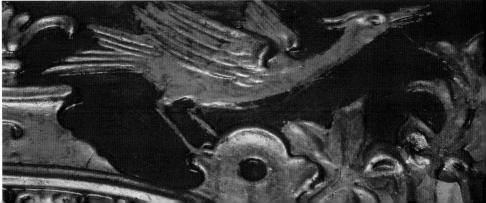

26. Trident House, 31 Dale Street

Among the row of symbolic reliefs on this elegant red-brick palazzo (in the style of an Italian civic building) is a Liver Bird with a long, looping neck holding an equally extensive sprig of seaweed in its bill (1). Other emblems include Lancashire roses and three lions from the county's coat of arms, Welsh leeks, English oaks and acorns.

Also visible on the exterior, the coronets of Lord Sefton. He was patron and first president of the Liverpool Reform Club, for whose Liberal businessmen the building was designed by local architect Edmund Kirby in 1879 (and operational until 1931). Inside the opulent interior are wine cellars, a library that once held 6,000 books and, facing a magnificent iron staircase on the first-floor landing, a slightly-damaged stained-glass window featuring another Liver Bird, streaked black with orange seaweed in its matching bill, inside a garland of fruit (2). Five adjacent windows contain crests with the archaic names Cambria, Hibernia, Lancastria, Scotia and Anglia.

27. No. 79 Tithebarn Street

Now part of John Moores University's Faculty of Health but originally an independent College of Commerce, this was the first such purpose-built institution of its kind in Britain, completed the year before the majestic Martins Bank on Water Street opened for business. Between a series of pilasters (columns projecting only slightly from the wall) with Ionic scroll-style capitals, reliefs of ancient and modern shipping (Liverpool's traditional means of commerce) flank a central panel of the city's coat of arms with a particularly hawkish Liver Bird, with short legs and a stiff tail at its centre (1). At the corner of Tithebran Street and Smithfield Street, two Liver Birds perched on fish support a vacant cartouche (2).

Founded in 1899, the college moved into its new home 30 years later. Faced in brick and Portland stone, the building was designed by city surveyor Albert D. Jenkins with sculptural decoration by a duo called Hooper & Webb. It was extended in 1954 and 1966 before the college combined with three existing schools of art, building and technology to form Liverpool Polytechnic in 1970.

Near this site in 1514 Lord Molyneux built the tithe barn (to hold one-tenth of his manor's annual produce) from which the street takes its name. His dynastic family, the Earls of Sefton, were second in power only to the Stanleys, Earls of Derby, in terms of power and influence in south Lancashire.

DEUS NOBIS HÆC OTIA FECIT

28. City Transport Offices, 24 Hatton Garden

A century's exposure to the elements has scored a faultline through the breast of the central Liver Bird (1) in this coat of arms above the building's main entrance. Upon a marble plaque in the foyer is another, smaller coat of arms below the words 'City of Liverpool Tramway Offices', commemorating the foundation stone laid by Lord Mayor John Lea on 12 September 1905 and acknowledging Thomas Shelmerdine as Corporation Architect and Surveyor (see his earlier Exchange Street Station, now Mercury Court on Tithebarn Street, and Everton Library). The building is now used as Mersey Travel's head office.

As well as the coat of arms on the exterior, there are two pairs of classically-dressed, allegorical female figures worked in Portland stone above the first-floor balconies. The first couple sit by a waterwheel and sailing ship (symbolising hydraulic power and maritime transport). The second pair are seated with a cogwheel, chain and caduceus (the wand carried by Mercury, god of commerce), a boat with a kestrel-like Liver Bird at its prow (2) and shaft of lightning (tramway electricity).

29. Youth Courts, Hatton Garden

From the rotund, tufty body of a grouse sprouts the long neck and strong legs of an emu but a proportionally tiny head and sawn-off tail. This strange, hybrid Liver Bird guards the Hatton Garden entrance to the city's juvenile courts, designed in 1897 by surveyor John Weightman (see his earlier Municipal Buildings and Liverpool Museum) as part of a group that included a bridewell on Cheapside, police headquarters and fire station (Hatton Garden, incidentally, is not named after the London street near Covent Garden but a village near Warrington where the Johnson brothers, who owned much of the land in this part of Liverpool, were born).

By then, Liverpool was taking positive steps to tackle the plight of child poverty among its working classes. As well as being one of the first cities to set up a special court exclusively for young offenders (on nearby Crosshall Street), it was among the first to control street trading by juveniles (1898) and organise special educational facilities for mentally and physically handicapped infants (1900). It even provided spectacles for poor children with bad eyesight.

30. Queensway Tunnel entrance, Old Haymarket

Sunken into a reservation near to the Queensway entrance, designed in breathtakingly modernist style by Herbert Rowse, is a large circular mosaic commemorating its opening in 1934. Bordered by a compass pattern, it features a map of the tunnel with its entrances, exits and ventilation towers on both sides of the Mersey, and various sailing and steam vessels on the river.

On the Liverpool bank is an impossibly elegant yellow, blue and grey Liver Bird (1) with wings like great canopies, a forked crest on its head, a tendrilled tail ending in three ornamental baubles and a long, thin wader's bill holding two wispy strands of seaweed. The mosaic is a copy of an original made from Venetian glass tesserae, which was positioned in a granite podium on the quartzite terrace on the tunnel roof behind the Old Haymarket entrance.

Archive photographs from the grand opening on 18 July, presided over by George V and Queen Mary and attended by 200,000 spectators, show the same bird on banners hanging from a ceremonial stage (a week-long celebration called the Festival of the Seven Lamps that consisted of parades, orchestras and organ recitals). 'It is a deep pleasure to us,' declared the king, 'to come here today to open for the use of men a thoroughfare so great and strange as this Mersey Tunnel, now made ready by your labour.

'I thank all those who have achieved this miracle. I praise the imagination that foresaw, the minds that planned, the skill that fashioned, the will that drove, and the strong arms that endeavoured in the bringing of this work to completion. May those who use it ever keep grateful thoughts of the many who struggled for long months against mud and darkness.'

An asymmetric relief of a Liver Bird (2), above an archway on the opposite side of the tunnel entrance, is an overhead variation of the mid-flight bird sculpted by Edmund C. Thompson and George C. Capstick for the George's Dock Building. The spade-shaped

tail and bill with rilled seaweed are clearly discernible, but the bird is deliberately mechanical looking, with wings more metallic than feathered and a tyred wheel for a body – symbolic of the tunnel's constant traffic. The same creature appears on the archways at the Birkenhead entrance and the walls of the obsolete branch exit at Birkenhead North (closed when traffic in the tunnel became too heavy), with perfunctory brick versions on the façades of the two ventilation towers on the Wirral side of the river.

Upon its opening, Queensway was the longest underwater road tunnel in the world and one of the 20th century's greatest feats of civil engineering. It measured 2.13 miles and required the excavation of 1.2 million tons of rock over five years (one ton every two minutes). One million bolts were used, along with 270,000 tons of concrete and 82,000 tons of cast iron to line the tunnel. On 3 April 1928, the pilot headings (small tunnels) from Liverpool met those from Birkenhead almost exactly under the centre of the river, the greatest divergence of line being one-and-a-half inches.

Queensway even has its own coat of arms, granted in 1952. Between two giant winged bulls ('symbolic of swift and heavy traffic') stand Apollo and Pluto, the gods of light and darkness. The shield between them contains a Liver Bird – now disfigured by exhaust fumes – and two stars below two lions holding a wheel. The motto underneath is Ripae Ulterioris Amore. It is from Virgil's *Aeneid* and means, 'In longing for the further bank'. Liverpool's traditional arms appears on the wall halfway through the tunnel, opposite that of Wirral.

31. Former Bank of Liverpool, 45 Victoria Street

Once a palatial branch of the Bank of Liverpool (whose headquarters were on Water Street), this is another building by architects Grayson & Ould, dating from 1882. The distinctive coat of arms on the south elevation high above Victoria Street (1) betrays their touch: no city motto this time, but the Neptune to the right seated on a bale of cotton (that most bankable of commodites), the upper bird in a seashell, and a beady-eyed fish head on a cartouche above. Compare this with the masterly coat of arms at 34-36 Castle Street by the same architects.

Either side of the arms are reliefs of Liver Birds (2) similar to those on no. 11 Dale Street but here topped by sheep's heads, another bird above Sir Thomas Street, decorative fish and dragons, and busts possibly of former bank managers or directors.

Established in 1831, the Bank of Liverpool was one of the first joint-stock banks (i.e. with an unlimited number of shareholders) set up in the aftermath of the Bank Act of 1826, itself the result of a major commercial and financial crisis caused by a spate of wars of independence in Latin America (which led to the collapse of 93 English and Welsh private banks).

Its first chairman was William Brown, son of the founder of the New York bank of Brown Brothers, Harriman & Co., and by 1882 its deposits had grown to £4 million. Eventually it would amalgamate with Martins Bank (later to become Barclays), but in 1901 it made international news with the arrest and trial of Thomas Goudie, an employee who embezzled £170,000 to pay off gambling

122

debts and was sentenced to 10 years' imprisonment. So, too, was professional boxer Richard Burge, who the judge declared had 'cheated and terrified Goudie whom the robbery benefited little'. Documentary footage about the case was found in the recently rediscovered archives of pioneering film makers Mitchell & Kenyon. It had been originally exhibited at the Prince of Wales Theatre on Clayton Square, three days after Goudie's arrest.

No. 45 Victoria Street is now Sir Thomas Street Hotel, named after the thoroughfare (in turn named after a former city mayor) that it occupies on the corner of Victoria Street. Formerly displayed in the hotel bar but currently in storage (awaiting a permanent home) is a magnificent bronze statue of a Liver Bird (3) over 3ft tall. It was a gift from the Royal Liver Friendly Society to the hotel's owners, who also run a bar at New Zealand House on Water Street. Both the latter building and the Royal Liver Building were designed by Walter Aubrey Thomas.

32. Union House, 21 Victoria Street

Over the iron staircase on the second-floor landing of this 1882 building (earmarked recently as a boutique hotel) is a plaster frieze depicting a scene from what appears to be a Caribbean tobacco plantation, with native peoples harvesting the plant's long leaves under the supervision of a pipe-smoking merchant. Above them, two unmistakable Liver Birds, holding decorative swags in their beaks, support a relief bust of a bearded Elizabethan gentleman in a ruff, possibly Sir Walter Raleigh.

In the ground-floor lobby is another frieze that illustrates the shipping of tea from China to Liverpool. This building, formerly called Palace Chambers, housed several provision merchants (sugar refiners were also tenants) in the late 19th century after Victoria Street was cut through as a spacious new commercial thoroughfare occupied by commodity exchanges, offices, warehouses and banks.

33. Municipal Buildings, Dale Street

Above the main entrance to Liverpool's erstwhile Council HQ (now its rates hall) is the city's official coat of arms (I). True to the heraldic description, the shield features a Liver Bird with dark, almost scale-like plumage, the webbed feet of a cormorant and 'in the beak a branch of Laver' (seaweed), flanked by two jovial, blue-eyed mermen with golden hair and 'sea-green mantles'. Of all the traditional coats of arms in the city, this is the only one in which the Neptune and triton appear to stare at each other across the central shield, and the latter does not blow his conch. Created by esteemed local sculptor Herbert Tyson Smith, this version dates from the 1920s and also appears on the Cenotaph at St George's Plateau, while a gilded replica of the bird in the shield can be found at Bluecoat Chambers.

Above the entrance, facing Dale Street, are three stone Liver Birds (2) projecting from corbels supporting the eave of the first-floor balcony. The bird in the middle rests its head on its breast, while those either side look up vigilantly. None have seaweed in their bills.

Now Grade II listed, the Municipal Buildings were designed in French Renaissance style by John Weightman, the Corporation Surveyor (see Youth Courts on Hatton Garden and Museum on William Brown Street) and erected in 1866 on the site of the old Saracen's Head coaching inn. At second-floor level, there are 16 allegorical figures ranging in subject from Britannia, Europe, Africa and the Americas to Shipping, Industry, Engineering, Science, Astronomy, the Arts and Commerce. Of the accompanying series of Corinthian columns, no two capitals are the same.

DEVS·NOBIS
HÆC·OTIA·FECIT

34. Municipal Annexe, 68 Dale Street

No expense spared inside or outside this former Conservative Club (then municipal offices, now a boutique hotel) that straddles half of the city block framed by Dale Street, Sir Thomas Street, Cumberland Street and Victoria Street. Along the north (facing Dale Street), east and west elevations are Liver Birds (1) projecting from corbels like those on the neighbouring Municipal Buildings, but here they have sprigs of seaweed in their bills. Between them, over the window bays, are a series of allegorical heads.

Inside, to the right, a compact, beautifully-coloured Liver Bird in a stained-glass window (2) with the city motto inscribed around its elliptic frame – perfectly at home in a French Renaissance interior that still has a stunning staircase and once boasted 600 upholstered chairs of carved oak and a lavish dining room that, reputedly, had 20 waiters. There were three rooms for billiards, too, and a couple for playing cards.

The Conservative Club was built in 1883 to the designs of George G. Holme and his nephew Francis Usher Holme, third-generation Liverpool architects, surveyors and engineers. From their practice on Crosshall Street, they also designed County Sessions House on William Brown Street and the Hahnemann Hospital on Hope Street as well as several police stations (see Anfield Road, Derby Lane and Lark Lane) and churches in Liverpool and North Wales. In 1836 George's elder brother Samuel had won the building contract for St George's Hall and became city mayor 16 years later.

35. Education Offices, 14 Sir Thomas Street

Two seismic seams separate the head and legs from the body of the century-old Liver Bird perched in profile in the pediment above the entrance of this suitably Dickensian building (1). In better condtition, facing each other across the first-floor windows, are two identical phoenix-like birds with customary sprigs of seaweed (2) in their sharp, curved beaks. Unusually, their full wingspan is portrayed but not their legs. Further sculptural decoration includes a group of figures called Knowledge Personified higher up on the pediment, and a boy and girl symbolising Science and Knowledge.

The granite, three-storey building was designed by Charles E. Deacon for the Liverpool School Board in 1898, two decades after the Elementary Education Act and a year after the opening of the Youth Courts on Hatton Garden. When Queen Victoria came to the throne in 1837, half of her subjects could not read or write, and midway through her reign an estimated 20,000 Liverpool children between the ages of five and 13 did not attend school.

The situation was highlighted in 1844 by German exile Friedrich Engels, whose *Condition of the Working Class in England* was a notorious social critique of daily life in the new industrial towns of Liverpool, Manchester and Birmingham, the 'workshop of the world'. Highlighting poverty, disease and child labour, it condemned the lack of compulsory education in England for children who worked throughout the week in factories, a tiny percentage of whom attended evening classes. 'It is really too much to expect a young person who has been at work for 12 hours to go to school between 9pm and 10pm,' wrote Engels. 'Most of those who do attend fall asleep.'

Four years later, he and Karl Marx wrote *The Communist Manifesto*. By 1870, a sustained campaign by philanthropists and reformers hastened an act of parliament making elementary schooling compulsory.

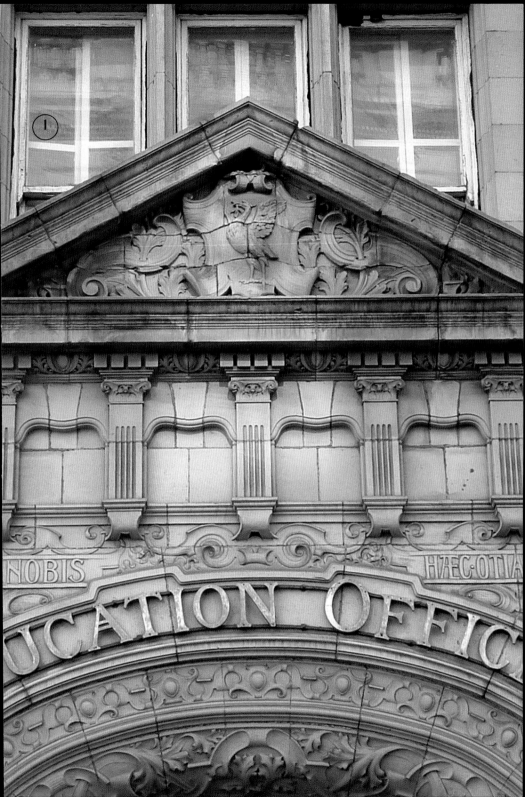

(1)

36. Conservation Centre, Whitechapel

A Liver Bird in a shield (1) on the Victoria Street façade of this great, sweeping building is one of several emblems of those cities served by the Midland Railway Line. This was its goods station – note the colossal doorways used to receive all manner of vehicles – built in 1850, now Grade II listed and housing the award-winning Conservation Centre that leads the way in laser cleaning and 3D digital scanning of public sculpture.

The statue in the foyer is the original, 15 ton statue of Liverpool sculpted in Rome by John Warrington Wood in 1875 and removed from the roof of the Walker Art Gallery in 1993 to prevent further deterioration (a replica now sits in its place). Carved from the flawless, white Carrara marble (after the town in Tuscany) so prized by sculptors over the centuries, she is a seated woman wearing a crown (indicating that she represents the city as a whole) and holding a trident (symbolic of Liverpool's maritime heritage). Beside her is a corroded brass Liver Bird (2) with a startlingly vertical crest, along with a cotton bale and propeller (commerce and the sea), palette, paint brushes and set square (arts and culture).

She and two statues of Michaelangelo and Raphael were hauled on rollers over four days from Warrington Wood's studio to Rome's railway station, where they were packed in massive timber crates, taken by rail to Livorno and thence by steamer to Liverpool. She was hoisted above the Walker through an opening behind the pediment, a process that took another three days.

37. Nos. 16-18 Whitechapel

A second glance is needed to notice these diminuitive, terracotta Liver Birds with dagger-like bills and mottled breasts in ornate shields, set within six panels above the first-floor windows of this substantial red-brick building framed by Whitechapel, Rainford Gardens and Stanley Street. It has been dated to the 1890s and was probably an office-warehouse complex associated with the provision trade that dominated the area around Mathew Street up to Victoria Street. Next door at 50-54 Stanley Street are the erstwhile premises of Hessey's, the celebrated Liverpool music store.

38. No. 12 Williamson Street

A petite Liver Bird in relief stands almost unnoticed in a shield festooned with decorative foliage over the arched entrance to this late 19th century building at the corner with Leigh Street. Just below the shield, upon the arch's keystone, is a carved head of a 'Green Man'.

For the past two decades the premises have housed a games arcade, but the 1902 edition of *Gore's Directory of Liverpool* (a forerunner of today's A-Z atlases) lists the occupants as Higgins, Eagle & Co, lace manufacturers. Their neighbours were tailors, drapers, silk and wool merchants, hosiers and Army and Navy contractors (supplying buttons, sashes, embroidery and other military regalia).

The street was created in the early 1800s and named after Richard Williamson. His family, according to an 1868 book by James Stonehouse entitled *The Streets of Liverpool*, 'have been denizens of Liverpool since Elizabeth's time, and whose descendants held property in which Williamson Square and Street arose, their country house being thereabouts'.

39. Compton House, 33-45 Church Street

One of the city's most charismatic coats of arms sits unnoticed by most Liverpudlians, silhouetted at the top of the most dominant building on Church Street, a survivor of both the 1941 Blitz and 50s redevelopment (and now home to Marks & Spencer). The seated Neptune's crown resembles the spines of an anemone, and his deep-set eyes and wispish beard give him a venerable, contemplative air. He and the triton to the right rest either side of a shell-like shield featuring a small Liver Bird with the city motto underneath but no second bird above.

Designed by Gerald de Courcy Fraser in 1867, the classically-styled building housed drapers J.R. Jeffrey & Co for 10 years until, after a fire, it was subdivided into W.H. Watts department store and the Compton Hotel, by which time its large sculpture of an eagle at the corner with Tarleton Street was a beacon for visiting and resident Americans in the city. The 1902 *New Illustrated Guide to Liverpool* comments that 'here American tourists flock in large numbers, being always certain of finding home life and probably meeting with friends and acquaintances. No class of people are so susceptible to the influences of domestic surroundings as the Americans, hence their patronage of the Compton, and their recommendation of its good qualities as a family hotel to their friends'.

40. No. 69 Church Street

A curly-tailed, crudely-rendered Liver Bird stands in the centre of an urn-like vessel in an aged stucco relief above the entrance to this building at the corner where Parker Street forks off Church Street. Either side of the urn's handles are two classical putti (young male nudes) seated upon grotesque winged tendrils and holding banners and swags of fruit in their hands.

Architectural experts have dated the building to around the 1880s. At the turn of the last century (as a framed photograph on the first floor testifies) it housed the Standard Raincoats & Weatherwear Shop. In 1820, the *Liverpool Mercury* newspaper carried an advertisement for a 'paper hanging manufactory' run by J. & J. Boswell on the same site. Today it is home to an optician's practice.

41. Bluecoat Chambers, School Lane

Four Liver Birds are arrayed around the city centre's oldest building, one of its select group of Grade I listed structures and arguably the most elegant.

Today the cornerstone of Liverpool's artistic and cultural life, Bluecoat Chambers was originally a school for orphans of seamen. An inscription in the front courtyard reads 'Dedicated to the promotion of Christian charity and the training of poor boys in the principles of the Anglican Church. Founded this year of salvation 1717.' When the school moved to Wavertree in 1906, the building was bought by soap magnate William Lever and transformed into the Bluecoat Society of Arts.

A golden Liver Bird greets visitors from the top of the wrought-iron gates of the main entrance (1), and a plaster copy (2) along with another dove-like bird (3) are set within pediments above doorways in the courtyard. A fourth gilded Liver Bird (4), inside a cartouche and surmounted by a cherub's head, is clearly the work of Herbert Tyson Smith. It is a replica of the web-footed bird in his city

arms on the Cenotaph and Municipal Buildings and a gift for the 'Bluecoat Brotherly Society' (reads the nearby plaque) to the Bluecoat Society of Arts.

A familiar figure in the 1920s and 1930s Liverpool, with his trademark trilby and bow tie, Smith had his studio at Bluecoat Chambers — initially as a pupil of the University's School of Art where he studied clay modelling, stone carving and plaster casting. His father had been a lithographic artist who made an address to Queen Victoria when she opened an International Exhibition in Liverpool in 1886.

Upon graduating, Smith worked with Charles J. Allen (famous for completing the series of allegorical panels outside St George's Hall in the 1890s) on portrait busts for the University and the Florence Nightingale Memorial on Princes Road, before finding fame for his own sculptural decoration on the Martins Bank Building and Cenotaph. He also cut the foundation stone for the Anglican Cathedral, his brother-in-law Edward Carter Preston supplying all of its sculpture.

42. No. 16 Wood Street

Libertas, as in freedom — of the press, in this instance. The Latin inscription below the Liver Bird on this building, situated at the corner with Roe Alley, recalls its original incarnation as the premises of the *Liverpool Mercury* newspaper, later to merge with the *Daily Post*. It was built in 1879, the year of Rorke's Drift and the Zulu Wars, at the same time that the Liberal Reform Club opened for business on Dale Street.

Amid bundles of fruit, the Liver Bird is perched on a horn and caduceus, symbol of peace and commerce, and wand of messenger god Mercury, whose sculpted head, complete with winged hat, also appears on the façade. A weekly digest of eight small pages, the *Mercury* was launched on 5 July 1811 by Egerton Smith, first from offices at Pool Lane then Lord Street and finally Wood Street. The country's first penny daily, however, was the *Liverpool Daily Post*, its first issue rolling off the presses (again from Lord Street) on 11 June 1855.

The *Daily Post's* inaugural editor was Michael James Whitty (see Anfield Cemetery), a Wexford man who had previously edited the *London & Dublin Magazine* then the weekly *Liverpool Journal* (founded in 1830), before becoming Liverpool's first Head Constable of the Police and Fire Brigade and ultimately returning to publishing. He was succeeded by Edward Russell, a Londoner who edited the paper for 59 years from 1869 to 1920 and was elevated to the peerage as Lord Russell of Liverpool. From its formative years, the *Daily Post* earned a reputation for liberalism, throwing in its lot with Gladstone and his Home Rule Bill (for a self-governing Ireland) and styling itself as an advocate of reform.

From new headquarters on Victoria Street, it launched the *Liverpool Echo* in 1879 and amalgamated with the *Mercury* in 1904, retaining the latter's office on Wood Street. In 1973 it moved to its current home (along with Royal Insurance) on Old Hall Street where modern Liver Bird motifs adorn the glass-plated entrance.

43. Nos. 43-47 Bold Street

Echoes of Halifax House on Fenwick Street, with two Liver Birds binding together a bundle of rods to form a fasces above the motto Vis Unita Fortior (Together We Are Stronger) on the façade of a former branch of the Liverpool Union Bank (latterly absorbed by Lloyds).

Here, the shield containing the two birds is supported above a ripple of intricately-carved waves by a Neptune and mermaid, with great, curled fish tails (and, sadly, faces and chests spoiled by guano). In his right hand, the Neptune grasps a frond of seaweed. In her left hand, the mermaid twists a strand of her own flowing, kelp-like hair.

This Italianate building was designed in 1885 by the familiar architectural duo Grayson & Ould, whose later Seymour Chambers on London Road – another branch of the bank – has similar sculptural decoration (see also their city coats of arms for rival banks at 34-36 Castle Street and 45 Victoria Street). By the turn of the 20th century, the branch had budged up to accommodate Sace de Paris at no. 43. The 1902 *New Illustrated Guide to Liverpool* carried an advertisement for this 'court artistic coiffeur, wig maker and perfumeur' that offered 'La Divine Bernhardt Vegetable Hair Dye in every natural shade, the celebrated lotion pro-phylactical treatment for the hair'. Its wigs, apparently, were 'made of Natural, Curly, and Waved Hair, and no heat of the Head or moisture of the atmosphere will remove the wave or curl'.

44. Old Bank, 66-68 Bold Street

A right-facing, long-billed Liver Bird stands in a decorative roundel above the first-floor window of this former Lloyds Bank building (now a bar) at the corner of Bold Street and Slater Street — unusual to see the bird featuring on the façade of a branch of a national bank as opposed to local, traditional and financial institutions like Martins, Leyland & Bullins, the Bank of Liverpool and Liverpool Union Bank. The emblematic Lloyds horse appears lower down, either side of the doorway.

Designed by George Hastwell Grayson (son of G.E. Grayson, see Victoria Chambers), the Portland stone-clad building dates from the late 1920s — when grand but simple Beaux Arts architecture was championed in the city — and the sculptural work has been attributed to Herbert Tyson Smith (see Martins Bank Building, Water Street).

45. Britannia Adelphi Hotel, Ranelagh Place

Above the arched ground-floor windows of this Beaux Arts masterpiece from 1914 are probably the flashiest Liver Birds in town — not just raising their wings but flexing them like Popeye with their taloned feet wide apart and seaweed in their long, straight bills. From a distance they also appear to be balancing coronets on their heads, both traditional (1) and in the shape of ships sails (2), but closer scrutiny reveals that each crown projects halo-like from the walls. The birds are the work of H.H. Martyn, a Gloucestershire firm of ornamental sculptors who also carved the reredos (altar screen) in the Anglican Cathedral

and carried out all the ornamental cast-iron work on the Queensway Tunnel's toll booths, lighting shafts and wall lamps, as well as manufacturing aircract components during World War One.

The building is the third hotel on this site, acquired by the Midland Railway Company in 1892. It was designed by R. Frank Atkinson, who had earlier created the Selfridges department store on Oxford Street in partnership with legendary Chicago architect Daniel Burnham. The Beaux Arts style is characterised by grandiose buildings with stone finishes and simple decoration, and exemplified in Liverpool by the Cunard Building at the Pier Head (completed two years later), the John Lewis (formerly George Henry Lee's and Bon Marché) store on Church Street, and Martins Bank and India Building on Water Street.

In its early 20th century heyday, the Adelphi was one of the most luxurious hotels in Europe, its decadent, marble-walled interiors (reception rooms, billiard rooms, banqueting suites, ballrooms and restaurants etc) designed to cater for transatlantic passengers on luxury liners. Its Sefton Suite is a replica of the First Class Smoking Lounge on the *Titanic*, and the decorations in the drawing room are based on those in a similar room at Versailles. Every room had a telephone, and the hotel became famous for its turtle soup. A 1914 souvenir book entitled *Adelphi Hotel: The History of a Great Enterprise* boasts that 'all the modern innovations of New York hotels of the highest grade here combine with solid British comfort, and that subtle air of refinement characteristic of a Parisian salon.'

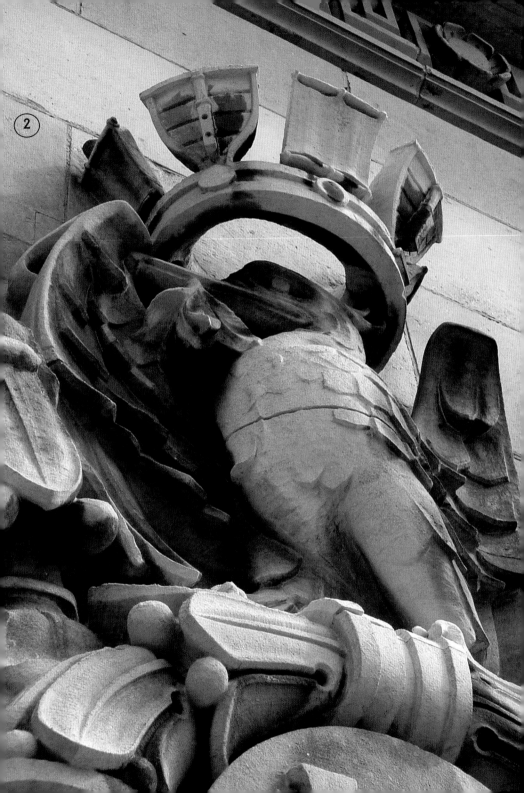

46. Central Hall, Mount Pleasant

Two extravagant cartouches on the façade of this Art Nouveau-Byzantine fantasy contain gilded reliefs of Liver Birds with fish, rather than seaweed, in their bills — symbols, traditionally, of disciples or newcomers to a faith.

Situated on the corner of Renshaw Street and Upper Newington, the building was originally the Central Hall of the Liverpool Wesleyan Mission, designed in 1905 by architects Bradshaw, Gass & Hope of Bolton, still in existence and a practice long associated with churches. The site was also the former meeting place of Liverpool's Unitarians, who had their roots in the non-conformist movement of the 17th century (like Islam and Judaism believing God was one and Jesus a prophet to be followed rather than worshipped). They were a powerful, free-thinking influence in the city, counting philanthropist and abolitionist William Roscoe among their congregation (he is buried in the adjacent gardens named after him) as well as the Harvey family, who established one of the city's earliest breweries that eventually became Higsons (see McHale's Bar on Lime Street and Blackburne Arms on Catharine Street). In 1899 they moved their church to Ullet Road in Aigburth.

47. McHale's Irish American Bar, 51-53 Lime Street

A very familiar Liver Bird found above pub signs all over Merseyside (see Blackburne Arms on Catharine Street) and the erstwhile symbol of the Higsons Brewery that existed for over 200 years. Plausibly proportioned with a draped peacock's tail, it is usually red but appears here in gold with emerald-green seaweed that resembles clover in its sharp beak, and the mechanistic wing feathers recall the plumage of the bird outside the former Liverpool Building Society at no. 1 Water Street. A miniature Statue of Liberty completes the pub façade's ensemble.

For years this was known simply as the American Bar. Until the 1920s it was located on the opposite side of Lime Street and became a haunt for US soldiers, sailors and airmen during both world wars. In the 1880s, however, it was officially the Midland Vaults, and 20 years earlier it was called the North British Hotel.

Up until it was acquired by Boddingtons in 1985, Higsons could lay claim to being the oldest established company of its kind in the city – founded by William Harvey at no. 64

Dale Street in 1780. Twenty years later it moved to purpose-built premises at 60 Cheapside before Harvey sold the business to Thomas Howard, who left his entire estate to his young bookkeeper David Higson.

By the late 19th century, an Irishman named Robert Cain was brewing his own 'superior ales and stouts' from a red-brick landmark building on Stanhope Street. Ultimately, he would build 200 pubs on Merseyside, including three of the most gloriously extravagant venues in Britain: the Philharmonic, Vines and Central. Knighted as Lord Brocket (his great-great-great grandson recently appeared on a reality television show), he died in 1907 and 3,000 mourners attended his funeral. In 1923, his brewery was taken over by Higsons.

Higsons prospered for another 60 years before it was acquired by Boddingtons and in turn sold to Whitbread, who announced the closure of the Liverpool brewery in 1990. After 12 redundant years, the Stanhope Street site was bought by brothers Ajmail and Sudarghara Dusanj – the first Indian family ever to own a British brewery – and the Cains name was spectacularly revived.

48. St George's Hall, Lime Street

Symbolism and civic pride unfettered inside this emphatic declaration of Liverpool's erstwhile status as the second city of the British Empire – a 490ft long, neoclassical concert hall designed in 1839 by Harvey Lonsdale Elmes at the ripe old age of 23.

Inside the colossal building, above a 7,737-pipe organ, the south end is dominated by a large semi-circular stained-glass window of the city's coat of arms (1) bordered by the emblems of England, Scotland and Ireland. Created by Liverpool company Forrest & Son, it depicts a Neptune and triton on a rocky outcrop at sea, the latter's green fish tail ending in a red, forked tip. Instead of a shield, the central Liver Bird stands within a mighty loop of black-and-yellow rope.

At the north end the stained glass is repeated, this time with St George and the Dragon as its subject. Below are three pairs of bronze doors with panels of foliage inhabited by front-facing Liver Birds (2) and incorporating tridents and the letters SPQL, an adaptation of the motto of Rome and meaning 'to the Senate and the People of Liverpool'.

⑤

These magnificent doors reappear three times along both sides of the hall. Above them, in arched niches between mighty columns of polished red granite, are more coats of arms (3) in colourful plasterwork (two each side) alternating with those of Lancashire and more depictions of St George and the Dragon. Over the latter, inside decorative bands of magnolia-white and cornflower-blue, stand single Liver Birds (4) with outspread wings (again two each side).

Up to the vaulted ceiling where the same Liverpool arms features six times in square plaster panels (5), again with the blazonry of Lancashire and St George but this time with the lion and unicorn of royalty at the centre. And down to the extravagant sunken floor of multicoloured tiles (covered with a removable wooden floor these days) upon which are two further coats of arms plus an array of maritime motifs and classical symbols of commerce and authority.

All of this interior decoration was overseen by Charles Robert Cockerell (see no. 1 Dale Street), who became chief architect of the

ongoing project when Elmes died from
consumption in the West Indies in 1849.

In comparision, the building's exterior is
austere. Dating from the 1880s are two series
of six allegorical panels either side of the
main entrance on the east façade (facing Lime
Street), carved by Thomas Stirling Lee, Charles
J. Allen and Conrad Dressler. Entitled 'The
Progress of Justice and National Prosperity',
they feature nude figures that caused a scandal
in their day. The second panel of the second
series, 'Liverpool Collects Produce and Exports
/ The Manufacturers of the Country', shows
a group of three female figures holding,
respectively, a large bundle, salver, sickle and
vessel embossed with a Liver Bird (6).

Now Grade I listed, St George's Hall
stands on a natural sandstone plateau that
was earmarked by Liverpool's Victorian elite
as a civic forum much like the Acropolis. On
a tour of Liverpool in 1851, Queen Victoria said
it was 'worthy of ancient Athens, the
architecture is so simple and magnificent'.
More recently, Princes Charles called it 'one
of the greatest public buildings of the last
200 years which sits in the centre of one of
Europe's finest cities'.

49. No. 139 Dale Street

On Trueman Street, between the arched portico and first-floor balcony of this elegant townhouse – reputedly the oldest in Liverpool – are three gold medallions containing, from left to right, a phoenix rising from flames, a sailor leaning on a rope and anchor, and a Liver Bird, atrophied by time but still discernible. Unusually, its body faces to the right but its head is turned to the left, seaweed clearly in its bill.

Dating from 1790, this was the distillery of John Houghton, who lived around the corner on Dale Street. At the time, Liverpool was a town of 70,000, there were public baths at George's Dock and Everton was a picturesque village. Records show that Houghton opened the Bull Inn on this site, and that he subsequently paid for the building of Christ Church on nearby Hunter Street (now the dual carriageway leading to Islington) at an estimated cost of £15,000.

This was the age of upheaval in the Old and New Worlds. In 1790 Edmund Burke wrote his *Reflections on the Revolution* in France, and the following year Thomas Paine published his riposte, *The Rights of Man*, inspired by America's declaration of independence in 1783. Liverpool, chief port of the Slave Trade, remained a solidly Tory town but strengthened its links across the Atlantic, capitalising on American patriotism with a pottery industry that produced and exported pieces celebrating the new nation.

Also in 1790, James Maury began a 39-year career as US Consul to Liverpool, one of his principle duties being to negotiate the release of drunken American sailors from the Tower on Water Street. His offices were on Paradise Street and he lived at no. 4 Rodney Street. One of his neighbours (at no. 35) was Pudsey Dawson, formerly colonel of the Royal Liverpool Volunteers (see its regimental colour in the Museum of Liverpool Life) who returned from the American conflict to found the School for the Blind on London Road, the country's first such institution.

In the same year, Banastre Tarleton, another erstwhile officer in the Volunteers, was elected to Parliament from Liverpool and led the reaction against the local anti-slavery movement championed by poet and man of letters William Roscoe, who had just moved from Mount Pleasant to the Dingle where, according to one of his verses, 'the linnet chirps his song'.

50. Cenotaph, St George's Plateau, Lime Street

A bronze cast of Herbert Tyson Smith's instantly recognisable coat of arms (see Municipal Buildings) appears at either end of this moving and very original war memorial on the plateau outside St George's Hall. Above the arms are inscribed the years of both world wars, and below are horseshoe-shaped wreaths. The detail of the arms is worth closer inspection — note the musculature of the mermen, the scales on the fish tail of the triton and the grooves on the conch.

Smith sculpted the arms between 1926 and 1930 (World War Two dates were added in 1946), probably carving his decorations for the Martins Bank Building at the same time. He was renowned for working closely with architects — in this case Professor Lionel Budden of the University — and preferred to work on site with only a small-scale sketch in clay. He won an open competition to provide the arms and reliefs for the Cenotaph, beating off 766 entrants despite submitting his design just 48 hours before the deadline. The same arms appear on the May Blitz Memorial unveiled at Anfield Cemetery in 1951.

His reliefs either side of the Grade II listed memorial are 31ft long. The east side (facing Lime Street) has lines of mourners in a cemetery — including Smith's wife and son and the sculptor himself at the far right with his hand in his jacket. An inscription reads 'To the men of Liverpool who fell in the Great War, and the victory that day was turned into mourning unto all the people.'

The west side features soldiers marching in rank, and scholars have remarked upon the sense of modernity in their rhythm. The inscription here reads 'As unknown and yet well known as dying and behold we love, out of the north parts...a great company and a mighty army.' It is taken from the *Book of Ezekiel*: chapter 38, verse 15.

51. World Museum, William Brown Street

Along the sandstone elevation facing William Brown Street is a traditional but simplified coat of arms (1), the Liver Bird in its huge central shield encircled by a loop of rope and a frieze entitled 'Liverpool Presiding over Commerce and Industry'. In the latter, a crowned female is flanked on her right by another woman with a length of rope, an apparently featherless Liver Bird (2) in a deteriorated condition and a youth in a canoe. On her left, a woman with a bale of cotton and child on a steamship.

Dating from 1860, all of the decorative carvings on this façade were by Frederick W. Pomeroy, a London-born sculptor who also supplied a statue of Frederick Stanley, 16th Earl of Derby, for the interior of St George's Hall and a William Gladstone statue for the House of Commons. In 1901 he designed the first Mr Universe statuette in America.

Now the main façade of the spectacular World Museum opened in 2005, this is the surviving exterior of the street's first classical building, realised in the same Greco-Roman style as St George's Hall (which had stood for 15 years). The architect was John Weightman (see his later Youth Courts on

Hatton Garden and Municipal Buildings on Dale Street).

Around the corner is a fine Edwardian annexe that originally housed the Central Municipal Technical College, designed in 1896 by E.W. Mountford (he worked on London's Old Bailey 10 years later). Above the entrance, facing Byrom Street, is a Liver Bird relief (3) with swags (festoons of flowers and fruit) above an arched window bay. Note the bird's swept-back crest, sharp beak, spade-shaped tail and raised right leg.

Inside, to the left and right of the splendid lobby, are two coloured bas-reliefs in lunettes (crescent-shaped spaces) depicting Liverpool's seafaring, industrial and artistic heritage. The relief on the left features a crowned, female personification of the city seated by a golden crest containing a stork-like Liver Bird (4), with a winged Mercury, sailor and child next to her and sailing ship in mid-distance. Both were designed by Pomeroy and painted by Londoner Robert Anning Bell, an important figure in the Arts & Crafts movement, who taught at Liverpool's nascent university in the late 1890s, designed mosaics for Westminster Cathedral and illustrated anthologies of Keats and Shelley. His painting Spring Revel (1916) hangs in the Lady Lever Gallery in Port Sunlight.

Also inside, a severely worn alabaster relief over a grand mantlepiece depicting a just discernible Liver Bird, wings lowered, in a crest (5) beneath a scallop shell supported by winged cherubs, with the scrolled city motto at its base.

52. Picton Library, William Brown Street

Scan the frieze along the entablature of this colonnaded, drum-shaped reading room, and spot 15 Liver Birds nesting amid thick foliage. Now part of Central Library, it was built in conjunction with the adjacent museum in 1879, modelled upon the British Museum's own reading room and named after James Picton, the Victorian architect who designed some of the most beautiful offices in Liverpool's business district (see Union Marine Buildings at 11 Dale Street).

It was the country's original free library and the first building in the city to have electric lighting. Along with two other reading rooms in the library, named Hornby and Oak, its historic collection boasts letters from Queen Victoria, Prince Albert, Benjamin Disraeli, William Gladstone, Florence Nightingale and George Stephenson, as well as American artist John James Audubon's massive and magnificent *Birds of America*, one of only 133 copies of the most valuable natural history book ever printed.

53. Walker Art Gallery, William Brown Street

Above the portico of this great neoclassical building, designed by H.H. Vale, is the female personification of Liverpool, constant and abiding
but actually a copy of the 1875
sculpture by John Warrington Wood now
in the Conservation Centre. By her side,
a Liver Bird made of aluminium which has been
anodised green to replicate the corroded brass
of the original.

Warrington Wood was one of a succession of
young Victorian sculptors from Britain who studied
and worked in Rome, creating heroic neoclassical
statues — considered to be ennobling and uplifting
— for wealthy patrons and their native towns and
cities back home. Similar works by his Liverpudlian
predecessors John Gibson and B.E. Spence are displayed in the Walker's ground-floor sculpture
gallery inside — along with casts of the Bassae
Marbles, brought to Britain by Charles Robert
Cockerell (see no. I Dale Street and St George's
Hall) and John Foster Junior, that almost certainly
inspired them.

This allegorical figure sits on the roof of the
first major public art gallery outside London —
named after local brewer and city mayor Andrew
Barclay Walker who paid for its construction — and
watches over a cobbled street honouring William
Brown, an Irishman with a cotton empire on both
sides of the Atlantic, who emigrated from
Ballymena to New York with his father in 1800 but
settled in Liverpool 12 years later.

54. County Sessions House, William Brown Street

The last of the William Brown Street set completed in 1884, more Renaissance in style than its neoclassical neighbours and featuring a graceful, dignified Liver Bird facing right within a garland of flowers on the yellow stone frieze opposite the Walker Art Gallery.

Today it is used by National Museums Liverpool for storage and administration, but originally it was home to the Quarter Sessions of West Derby Hundred of the County of Lancaster — a place in Liverpool to hold trials for non-capital offences — whose arms are found in the main façade's pediment (see Victoria Chambers on Castle Street and the Police Station on Old Swan's Derby Lane).

The architects were F & G Holme, the local duo behind the Conservative Club on Dale Street and Hahnemann Hospital on Hope Street.

County Sessions is a wonderfully complex building. There are four separate entrances: the spectacular front door for magistrates and barristers, a not-quite-as-grand side-door on Mill Lane for solicitors and witnesses, an ordinary door at the back for members of the public, and a brooding iron gate on the east side for prisoners. Inside, the arrangement of stairs and corridors was ingeniously designed to ensure that these four categories of user did not have to meet until they confronted each other in the courtrooms.

55. Nos. 34-48 London Road

Two sculptures of crestless, front-facing Liver Birds with fleecy, puffed-out chests and stubby bills with seaweed stand in bulrushes between twin window arches above the entrance of this erstwhile drapers shop (how much more conspicuous they would be in different colours to the building's stucco exterior). Close to each are braces of lions' heads, and there are dragons in the pediments high above.

In 1901 these were the new premises of Ray & Miles general house furnishers, established in 1864 with branches on Church Street and Bold Street. As the main artery into town from the south and east, London Road was an equally important shopping thoroughfare, famous for its shoe shops and formerly home to Owen Owen, the great department store founded by one of Liverpool's greatest Welsh sons.

56. Seymour Chambers, 92-100 London Road

Along the curved corner with Seymour Street, two agitated Liver Birds, flanked by mermen, face each other and tighten a bundle of rods with their bills above the motto 'Vis Unita Fortior'. Like nos. 43-47 Bold Street and Halifax House on Fenwick Street, it is a branch of the Liverpool Union Bank, almost certainly designed by Grayson & Ould (in 1890) and again with carvings of roses, thistles, leeks and shamrocks to signify the four nations of the British Isles.

Further similarities with the Bold Street branch include the boiling waves beneath the motto, and the absence of an 'Eastern crown gold' and banner from the Neptune's head and left hand (presumably to differentiate him from the version on the city's official coat of arms). Instead, he and the triton use their free arms to lean against the crest containing the birds.

57. Pembroke Place, 106 London Road

On the next corner up from Seymour Chambers stands this fine red-brick building with an octagonal clock tower, erected for the Liverpool Furnishing Company in 1899 and attributed to architects W. Hesketh & Co. Above the entrance, at its corner with Hart Street, is a small terracotta Liver Bird relief in a medallion and crest balanced upon a genial allegorical head.

The decorative sculpture was supplied by the exotically-named Jabez Thompson of Northwich, famous for his terracotta busts of Victorian social commentator and building conservationist John Ruskin, and whose family owned the last surviving salt works in Britain.

58. Royal Infirmary, Pembroke Place

On the octagonal twin towers above the old outpatients department of the Liverpool Royal Infirmary are three terracotta panels, each depicting an angel and a crowned Liver Bird with the inscription 'Beati Misericordes' meaning 'Blessed Companion'.

Designed in 1909 by J. Francis Doyle (the architect behind Royal Insurance's gold-domed building on Dale Street), this was an extension to Alfred Waterhouse's Infirmary that had opened in 1889. In the same decade Liverpool-born Waterhouse, the Victorian equivalent to Sir Norman Foster, had also designed the nearby Victoria Building for the budding University and the Prudential Assurance Building on Dale Street. These, as well as his earlier North Western Hotel on Lime Street (and Natural History Museum in London), mark the high point of Gothic Revival architecture in Britain.

Like the Hahnemann Hospital on Hope Street (raised around the same time), the Infirmary was built to a plan based on Florence Nightingale's guiding principles – small but spacious and well-ventilated 'pavilion' wards to combat infectious diseases. Waterhouse had consulted Nightingale in 1885, and 20 years earlier William Rathbone VI had been inspired by her to establish a School of Nursing. She was commemorated in stained glass in the Infirmary's chapel.

In 1978 the Infirmary was replaced by the Royal Liverpool University Hospital across the road and more recently its oupatients department was converted into the Foresight Centre, providing organisations with access to the University's technological expertise.

59. Victoria Building, Brownlow Hill

Terracotta, sandstone and, above all, red brick dominate the Gothic façades of the oldest building on the University of Liverpool campus, designed by Alfred Waterhouse in 1887 (see his Royal Infirmary from the same year) and christened in honour of the reigning monarch.

The clock tower features Liver Birds with lowered and elevated wings (the former resembling a heron), inside and above a shield with the city motto below (1). Behind the tower, inside the quandrangle, are reliefs of top-heavy Liver Birds on buttresses (2) and two interesting coats of arms (3) on its east-facing façade. The first features a Liver Bird below a flower, hanging sheep, and bees on a globe, suggestive of veterinary science and animal husbandry (one of today's faculties) above the inscription 'Olim Armis Nunc Studiis' (Once By Arms, Now By Study). The second has the University's traditional three birds surrounding an open book with the motto 'Fiat Lux' (Let There Be Light) above the inscription 'Haec Otia Studia Fovent', in reverence to the city's own motto and translating as 'These Gifts Foster Learning'.

Completed in 1892, the Victoria Building was the Liverpool 'branch' of the Victoria University of the North of England, which also included colleges in Manchester and Leeds. The Liverpool college had been founded 10 years previously with a principal, 10 professors, and 93 students, its roots in both the much earlier Mechanics Institute and the more recent Medical School attached to the Royal Infirmary. In 1903 it was established by royal charter as the fully independent University of Liverpool.

Currently in the midst of a refurbishment, by 2008 the Victoria Building will house an exhibition of the University's considerable art treasures — including the gallery from Abercromby Square that boasts the most significant collection of wildlife paintings by John James Audubon outside the US.

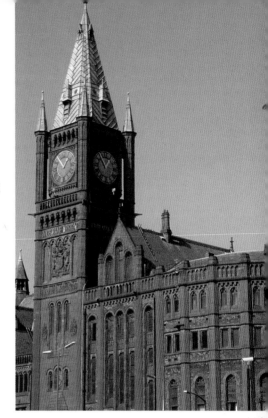

(2)

60. University of Liverpool Precinct

What was once a small group of academic buildings with the Victoria clocktower at its centre is now an 85-acre site encompassing one of the leading research universities in the country, renowned for its world-class teaching, with six faculties, 3,000 international students and architecture ranging from classical to gothic to modern.

Its coat of arms comprises an open book with the motto 'Fiat Lux' (Let There Be Light) between three silver Liver Birds that represent Liverpool as a seaport, seat of a bishopric and founder of University College. The silver colour of the birds is the emblem of purity.

In Abercromby Square, the arms appear on a stone plaque (1), flag (2) and iron gate pier (3), and they are repeated impressively in Portland stone (4) on the exterior of the Sherrington Buildings on Ashton Street, home to the Faculty of Medicine. With the exception of the flag, the trio of birds on all of these arms are clearly the work of artist-sculptor Herbert Tyson Smith — their prototype being the upper bird, atop the

central shield, on his city coat of arms (see Municipal Buildings).

The University's arms are also found in stone on brickwork on the Herdman Building on Brownlow Street (opposite the west façade of the former Royal Infirmary), housing the Laboratories of Geology. Here, they are presented in a cartouche, upon which perches another Liver Bird (5) flanked by swags and torches (symbolic of enlightenment) mounted on fasces (representing power).

Among the notable scholars who have walked along these precincts: Professor Oliver Lodge, who made the world's first public radio transmission in 1894 and demonstrated the use of X-ray photography two years later; Ronald Ross, who researched the origins of malaria, became head of the Liverpool School of Tropical Medicine in 1899 and won the Nobel Prize; Sir James Chadwick, who discovered the neutron in 1936 and was another Nobel Laureate; Allan Downie, professor of bacteriology from 1943 to 1966 and instrumental in the eradication of smallpox; and Dr Robert Minnitt, honorary lecturer in anaesthesia from 1933 to 1947, who developed the use of gas and air in childbirth.

61. John Moores University, Mount Pleasant

At the corner with Hope Street, this is one of numerous sites around the city at which this modern Liver Bird motif, unusually facing to the right and with a distinctively perpendicular bouquet of seaweed in its sharp beak, appears. Rendered here in metal and elsewhere in glass (e.g. Avril Robarts Centre on Tithebarn Street), it is designed to be easily recognisable as a building of the John Moores University established in 1992.

Now one of the largest universities in the country with six faculties, 24,000 students and strong disciplines in digital technology and space exploration, the John Moores University takes its name from Sir John Moores, founder of the Littlewoods shopping empire synonymous with the city for over 80 years, and a latter day philanthropist.

62. Back Maryland Street

Two angular Liver Birds, recalling the erstwhile Liverpool Polytechnic, survive in excellent condition on elliptical, gold-painted grilles upon iron gates at either end of this closed street running parallel with Hardman Street. Facing right and holding inverted sprigs of seaweed in their beaks, they are clearly precursors to the John Moores University bird that appears at various sites in the city centre.

The thoroughfare is bookended by Baltimore Street and South Hunter Street – all of them laid out and christened in the 18th century by a merchant called Mr Hunter who was engaged in the Virginia tobacco trade. The gardens of his house on nearby Mount Pleasant extended to this site, today home to John Moores University's Student Union and still a bucolic retreat in the heart of the city.

63. Hahnemann Hospital, 42 Hope Street

A beautiful building, recently sold by John Moores University (formerly housing its School of Art and Design) but brought to Liverpool in 1887 by the combined efforts of an eccentric German physician, Crimean War nurse and billionaire sugar importer. Its Grade II listed exterior is composed of red Ruabon brick (after its source near Wrexham), white stone, terracotta and Welsh slate (on the roofs), and the decorative sculpture rewards closer scrutiny.

Either side of the arch above the main entrance are small reliefs of Liver Birds facing each other within ornate roundels (1 and 2), with another bird on the pediment high above surrounded by two sabre-toothed cats with serpent tails and a fabulously grotesque fish (3). On the north elevation's pediment (facing Hope Place) is an improvised coat of arms featuring a Liver Bird in a crest surmounted by more grimacing fish and supported by serene, fish-tailed cherubs (4).

The architects were George and Francis Holme of Crosshall Street (see their Municipal Annexe at 68 Dale Street, built four years earlier), and the shape and style of the birds suggest that the same team had a hand in Venice Street Board Schools in Anfield, erected 12 months earlier in 1886.

This was one of the earliest homeopathic hospitals in Britain, paid for by Henry Tate, philanthropist, sugar magnate and founder of the eponymously-named art gallery. In an overcrowded city stricken by outbreaks of cholera and typhus, he was part of a progressive merchant class disillusioned by established medical practices like bloodletting and

fascinated by new holistic therapies. Their champions were Samuel Hahnemann, a German doctor working from the ancient Greek principle that 'like cures like' (e.g. taking quinine to combat malaria) and Florence Nightingale, who had lectured in Liverpool about the causes of 'hospital diseases' (confined wards, poor light and ventilation etc) and how to combat them. It was upon her principles — wards with high ceilings and large windows, beds well apart and a ventilation system using 'self-acting suction power' to remove foul air — that the hospital was built.

A reclusively shy man, Tate declined to attend the grand opening. His speech, read out by a deputy, proclaimed 'the great wish of my heart...to present to the inhabitants of Liverpool, without distinction of class or opinions, the Hahnemann Hospital'. The *Daily Post* noted his 'princely generosity' in providing 'a model modern hospital, combining the utmost comfort with all the recent adaptations for the benefit of patients which hygienic science can suggest'.

In time, Tate received the freedom of the city, Hahnemann also had a road named after him in Anfield, and a memorial to Florence Nightingale was erected on Princes Road.

64. Blackburne Arms, Catharine Street

The original and ubiquitous Higsons Liver Bird (see McHale's Irish American Bar on Lime Street), here recently repainted gold from its more usual trademark red, perched above the sign of this handsome public house and hotel at the corner with Falkner Street. It is named after John Blackburne, mayor of Liverpool in 1760 – although the new pub sign displays the arms of the Lancashire town of the same name.

Situated in the University quarter, the building has been described as the most architecturally perfect alehouse in the city, detailed to fit in with the area's adjoining Georgian terraces. It dates from 1927 and the architects were Harold E. Davies & Son. The son in question was Harold Hinchcliffe Davies, a graduate of the Liverpool School of Architecture, who specialised in designing pubs. He and his family appear in a photographic portrait by Edward Chambre-Hardman (whose time capsule Rodney Street home is now a National Trust museum), taken in an Avignon garden café a year before the Blackburne Arms was built.

BLACKBURNE ARMS HOTEL

ARTE ET LABORE

ENSUITE ROOMS
0151 707 1249

65. Anglican Cathedral, St James Road

Liver Birds carved from English oak stand sentinel at the end of every choir stall in the chancel of this sandstone and stained-glass leviathan. Note their celestial wings, stern brows and mighty hooked beaks and talons. In an official handbook from 1924, half-a-dozen carvers are listed among the individuals and firms 'principally concerned with the building of the Cathedral' (including sculptors, masons, labourers, bricklayers, scaffolders, joiners, blacksmiths and embroiderers). But H.G. Ratcliff is generally acknowledged as the principal woodworker.

At 101,000sq ft, this is the fifth largest cathedral in the world and its 13 mighty bells possess the heaviest and highest ringing peal in the world. Designed by Giles Gilbert Scott, a 23-year-old Roman Catholic, it was 100 years old on 19 July 2004 but took the best part of 75 years to complete.

OUT OF TOWN

66. Vermont House, Stanley Road, Bootle
67. Town Hall, Oriel Road, Bootle
68. Langton Castle, Regent Road, Bootle
69. Sherlocks Bar, Regent Road, Vauxhall
70. L & Y Railway viaduct, Great Howard Street
71. Leeds & Liverpool Canal, Vauxhall
72. Gordon Institute, Stanley Road, Kirkdale
73. Fire Station, Westminster Road, Kirkdale
74. Everton Library, St Domingo Road, Everton
75. Venice Street Board Schools, Anfield
76. Liverpool Football Club, Anfield
77. Old Police Station, Anfield Road
78. Anfield Cemetery
79. Alsop High School, Delf Lane
80. Old Bank, 475 Queens Drive
81. Barclays Bank, Mill Lane, West Derby
82. Melwood, West Derby
83. Old Police Station, Derby Lane, Old Swan
84. Old Bank, 611 West Derby Road, Tuebrook
85. Seamen's Orphanage, Newsham Park
86. The Belmont, Belmont Road, Anfield
87. Ogden's, Boundary Lane, Kensington

88. Brougham Terrace, West Derby Road
89. Old Bridewell, Harper Street, Kensington
90. Old Bank, Deane Road, Kensington
91. Grosvenor Hotel, Lodge Lane
92. Granby Street Board Schools, Toxteth
93. Princes Boulevard, Toxteth
94. High Park Street reservoir, Dingle
95. Old Savings Bank, 147 Park Road, Toxteth
96. Brunswick Station, Sefton Street
97. Toxteth Annexe, Aigburth Road
98. Old Bank, Aigburth Road, Aigburth
99. Sefton Park, Aigburth
100. Old Police Station, Lark Lane
101. Unitarian Church, Ullet Road, Aigburth
102. Picton Road Baths, Wavertree
103. Blue Coat School, Wavertree
104. Memorial, Holy Trinity, Wavertree
105. Calderstones Park, Allerton
106. Fountain, Grange Lane, Gateacre
107. Birkenhead Brewery, Woodside
108. Old Bank, 72 King Street, Wallasey

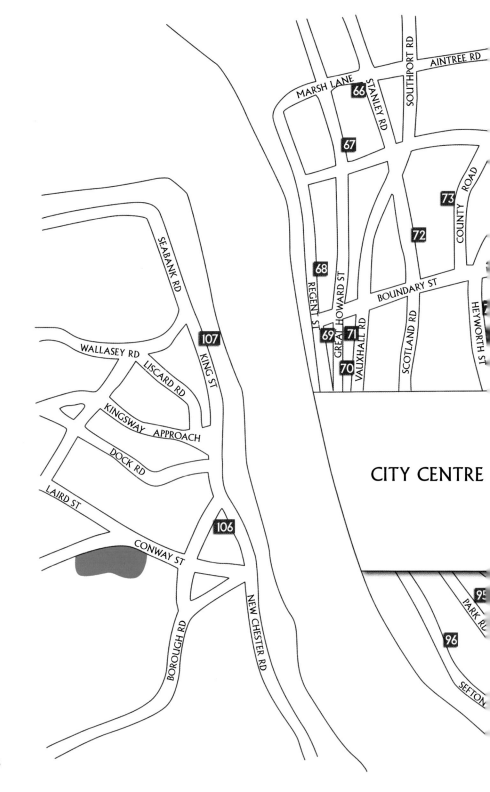

CITY CENTRE

EAST LANCS RD

M57

80

81

82

TOWNSEND LANE

BRECK RD

76 77

SHEIL RD

84

QUEENS DRIVE

WEST DERBY RD

86

87

85

88

83

89

PRESCOT RD

90

EDGE LANE

M62

LODGE LANE

PICTON RD

102

92 91

103 104

101

RD

SMITHDOWN RD

ULLET RD

105

MENLOVE AVENUE

106

100

99

MATHER AVENUE

AIGBURTH RD

98

66. Vermont House, Stanley Road, Bootle

The powerful, upright Liver Bird from no. 1 Water Street makes a large-scale reappearance upon the concrete exterior of a brutalist building, that housed first the Liverpool Building Society then the housing and social services department of the old Sefton Metropolitan Borough Council.

Today technically in South Sefton, in the 17th century the seaside hamlet of Bootle belonged to Colonel John More, a fierce Parliamentarian during the English Civil War and one of the signatories to the death warrant of Charles I (Old Hall Street in the city centre is named after one of his properties). In 1724, his family sold the land to the Stanleys, Earls of Derby, after whom this thoroughfare and several others are named. In turn they sold great tracts for dockland and industrial development, although much of the subsequent Victorian landscape was destroyed by air raids during World War Two.

67. Town Hall, Oriel Road, Bootle

Liverpool's coat of arms is just one of almost two-dozen shields decorating the exterior of this Grade II listed building, built in 1882 and now occupied by Sefton Metropolitan Borough Council. The other towns (all historically in Lancashire) are Accrington, Ashton-under-Lyne, Barrow-in-Furness, Blackburn, Bolton, Burnley, Bury, Chorley, Clitheroe, Darwen, Lancaster, Manchester, Oldham, Preston, Rochdale, St Helens, Salford, Southport, Stalybridge, Warrington and Wigan.

Among the memorabilia inside are ensigns and bells from warships based at nearby Gladstone Dock, and captained by Battle of the Atlantic hero Frederick 'Johnny' Walker. A strategically-important hub of factories and transportation links, the town was heavily bombed during Merseyside's infamous May 1941 Blitz, with 75 percent of its dwellings destroyed or damaged and half of its commerce incapacitated.

Prior to the development of its dock system between 1862 and 1927 (mainly to handle timber), Bootle was noted for its sand hills, sea-bathing amenities and natural springs from which water was pumped to Liverpool (see Westminster Road Fire Station). It was also a last stop along the Leeds and Liverpool Canal to the terminus at Old Hall Street.

68. Langton Castle, Regent Road, Bootle

A sandstone Liver Bird stands in a hanging shield above the entrance to this derelict public house at the northern limit of the Central Docks, where it adjoins Liverpool Freeport. The pub takes its name from the adjacent dock opened in 1879 and noted at the turn of the last century for its huge, 100-ton hydraulic crane.

Vauxhall was a ghetto for immigrants of many nationalities, and watering holes like the Langton Castle would have welcomed dockers, seamen, immigrants and emigrants amid a cacophony of sounds and smells, sails and rigging, and smoke and steam in this vicinity, with human traffic transferred to and from ships, stagecoaches and trains, and every imaginable cargo (cotton, coffee, rum, molasses etc) stored in warehouses and shifted on horse-drawn drays and canal barges.

Herman Melville, author of *Moby Dick*, sailed as a cabin boy from New York to Liverpool in 1839 and later wrote 'From the various boarding houses, each distinguished by gilded emblems outside – an anchor, a crown, a ship, a windlass or a dolphin – proceeds the noise of revelry and dancing; and from the open casements lean young girls and old women, chattering and laughing with the crowds in the middle of the street.

'Every moment strange greetings are exchanged between old sailors who chance to stumble upon a shipmate, last seen in Calcutta or Savannah, and the invariable courtesy that takes place upon these occasions, is to go to the next spirit vault, and drink each other's health.'

There was little distinction between spirit vaults, beer houses, gin palaces, and wine and spirit dispensaries in the mid 19th century. Under the collective umbrella of licensed premises in Liverpool, they numbered over 2,800 in 1865.

69. Sherlocks Bar, Regent Road, Vauxhall

A tiled replica of the Town Hall floor's coat of arms adorns one of the few surviving public houses along this stretch of the Central Docks (like the Baltic Fleet and Coburg pubs on the South Docks), now a shadow of their former selves.

The sandstone, granite and cast-iron foundations for Liverpool's integrated dock system, one of the wonders of the industrial world, were laid by Yorkshireman Jesse Hartley. In 1824 he was appointed as the world's first professional dock engineer and proceeded to build, enlarge or remodel no fewer than 26 docks – including the signature Albert (to handle high-value bonded goods), Waterloo and Trafalgar (both grain), Brunswick, Huskisson and Canada (all timber), Stanley (tobacco) and Clarence (for steamships) – in architectural styles ranging from Greek Revival to Gothic. His work was continued, and more massive warehouses added by his successors G.F. & A.G. Lyster.

Running alongside Regent Street, all the way from the city centre and up to Bootle, is Hartley's fortress-like Dock Wall, rising 18ft high in places and punctuated by colossal gatepiers. The novelist Nathaniel Hawthorne, American consul in Liverpool in the 1850s, likened it to the Great Wall of China. Similarly, an overhead railway – dubbed the Docker's Umbrella – once ran the length of this area until its closure in 1956.

70. Lancashire & Yorkshire Railway viaduct, Great Howard Street

An oval stone plaque either side of this viaduct between Great Howard Street and Pall Mall marks one of the many engineering achievements of John Hawkshaw. Dated 1849, it features a Liver Bird that faces right, as well as the inscribed names of Hawkshaw and contractors McCormick & Holmes.

Built for the Lancashire & Yorkshire Railway, the viaduct was originally over a mile long with 117 arches and ran parallel with the river all the way to Tithebarn Street (see Exchange Street station). Twenty years earlier the Liverpool & Manchester Railway, engineered by George Stephenson, had become the world's first purpose-built passenger railway.

Yorkshire-born Hawkshaw had an astonishing career. Prior to this contract, he spent three years as a copper-mining engineer in Venezuela, built a railway from Leipzig to Dresden, and assisted the legendary Jesse Hartley with the Albert Dock. In later life he designed stations for London's Charing Cross and Cannon Street, surveyed railways in Russia and India, and was invited by Said Pasha, the viceroyal of Egypt, to report on the feasibility of a Suez Canal. At the latter's grand opening in 1869, French engineer Ferdinand de Lesseps declared that 'the accomplishment of this great enterprise' was owed mainly to Hawkshaw. He was knighted in 1873.

The whole area bordered by Great Howard Street and Leeds Street has lain quiet for decades, but in the mid-19th century it was Liverpool's chief arrival point — a nexus of rail, the Leeds & Liverpool Canal (opened in 1830 and now filled in at Pall Mall) and Princes Dock landing stage. As such, city-centre maps from the period tend to focus here rather than, say, the Pier Head and Albert Dock.

71. Leeds & Liverpool Canal, Vauxhall

A serene Liver Bird, wings tucked down and ragged crest along its exaggerated, S-shaped neck, stands in relief upon a series of circular cast-iron plaques either side of three road bridges spanning the Leeds & Liverpool Canal where it runs parallel to Vauxhall Road.

The plaques at Leigh Bridge (1), near to Eldonian Village, mark the structure's re-erection by the city's Health Committee in 1861 when future mayor Thomas Dover was its chairman. The Boundary Street Bridge (2)

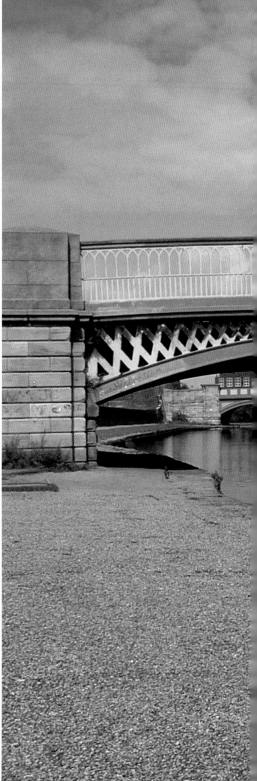

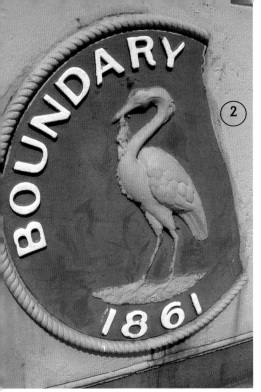

was widened in the same year, while the third bridge at Sandhills (3) was erected by the Corporation of Liverpool in 1874, with its plaques commemorating Andrew Barclay Walker as mayor (see his gallery on William Brown Street), John Stopford Taylor as chairman of the Health Committee and George Frederick Deacon as engineer (see High Park Street reservoir in Dingle). Similar plaques appear upon the recently refurbished Brunswick Station along the southern waterfront.

Terminating at Old Hall Street, the 127-mile canal had been fully operational since 1816, providing a conduit to Liverpool and overseas for raw materials (coal, iron, steel and salt), and finished goods (textiles and pottery) from the industrial heartlands of the North and Midlands. With the gradual ascension of rail over waterway, the loading basins clustered around its edge were filled in and replaced by storage sheds, although several of its canal-side inns (the equivalent of stagecoach posting houses) survived well into the 20th century.

Old photographs depict children swimming in the canal where it appears to steam, thanks to warm water discharged back into its course by adjacent factories. The threat of disease in such circumstances — not to mention the cholera and dysentery epidemics unleashed by the overwhelming influx of Irish refugees to the Vauxhall area in the mid-19th century (142,000 people to each square mile) — led to the founding of the Health Committee that built the bridges and appointed the country's first medical officer, William Duncan, to combat insanitary housing conditions among the poor.

72. Gordon Institute, Stanley Road, Kirkdale

A small, bushy-tailed Liver Bird stands in a crest next to a carved bust of Queen Victoria and the Lancashire coat of arms, to commemorate the opening of Liverpool's first purpose-built working-lads institute (now a community centre) in 1886. It was erected by farming businessman William Cliff in memory of his young son, and named after military hero General Gordon who had died at Khartoum a year earlier. Four years later, a similar establishment was opened further south in Dingle by West India merchant and former mayor Bernard Hall in honour of his deceased daughter Florence.

Originally a Norse settlement, Kirkdale was owned by Colonel John More in the 17th century (see Vermont House in Bootle). The nexus of major routes to Liverpool from Bootle and Everton, it acquired a gaol in the 1820s that attracted vast crowds for public executions. Like Dingle, it metamorphosed into a densely-populated dockside district in the second half of the 19th century, mainly due to Irish immigration.

73. Old Fire Station, Westminster Road, Kirkdale

A large, thick-set Liver Bird in sandstone, wings oustretched and chest inflated, stares vigilantly from this former fire station at the corner of Westminster Road and Bradewell Street, not far from the Central Docks. Note its long, square tail, cockatoo's crest and the curious tuft on its chest. Dating from 1885, it remains in good condition apart from a cheese-wire fissure between its head and body.

The building was erected almost 30 years after Liverpool's fire brigade had been recognised as a separate entity from its police force (hence the term 'fire bobbies'), with the opening of a dedicated station on Hatton Garden (see Youth Courts). The 1880s saw a gradual transition in the city's fire-fighting service from horse-drawn carts to steam engines, with water being pumped not just from Corporation wells in Bootle and Copperas Hill but the Rivington reservoir near Chorley (see High Park Street, Dingle) to ensure a supply of 70 million gallons a day.

Historians claim that the Great Fire of London in 1666 was a significant catalyst for Liverpool's growth, with merchants escaping the capital to settle in the blossoming, Atlantic-facing port. Liverpool's own series of dockside infernos in 1816, 1823, 1833 and 1842, preceded the formation of the Royal Insurance Company and the passing of a Fire Prevention Act that laid down standards for future warehouse con-struction. In the early 1970s, the respective fire brigades of Liverpool, Birkenhead, Bootle, Wallasey and Southport were merged into the Merseyside County Fire Brigade (now Service) with its headquarters at Hatton Garden and then on Bootle's Bridle Road.

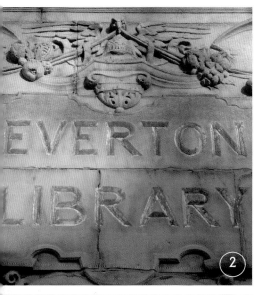

74. Everton Library, St Domingo Road, Everton

There is an Ozymandian air of antiquity to the handsome but crumbling coat of arms (1) on this forgotten building, on the long stone spine that constitutes the city's northern brow. Its weathered Liver Birds are barely visible, and only the faces of the Neptune and triton are in decent condition. Also on the sandstone façade is a front-facing and hawk-like Liver Bird (2), wings extended and a length of vine in its beak amid bountiful fruit. Further sculptural decoration includes books and torches (of knowledge).

Designed by Thomas Shelmerdine (see his City Transport Offices and Exchange Street Station) and erected in 1896, this building housed both a library and a technical college, serving what had grown from a prosperous and picturesque village inhabited by merchants made rich from commerce in the Caribbean, to a densely-populated suburb of Liverpool crammed with terraced housing built by Welsh immigrants. It had separate reading rooms for ladies, boys and the general public, and a plaque inside commemorates a former student of the college who won a Victoria Cross during World War One.

At the opening ceremony, the library was described as being in 'the immediate vicinity of that formerly occupied by a beacon. This beacon guided vessels, richly laden with merchandise, up the Mersey, and it is hoped that the building which has taken its place will guide the residents of Kirkdale and Everton to where the rich stores of knowledge lie'.

75. Venice Street Board Schools, Anfield

A sprightly little Liver Bird, head tilted upwards and teardrop-shaped seaweed in its beak, stands in a pediment dated 1886 at the top of this red-brick building off Walton Breck Road. The bird bears a close similarity to that on the old Gordon Working Lads Institute in Kirkdale erected the same year, and those on the Hahnemann Hospital on Hope Street built in 1887.

Schools like this, and the one on Granby Street in Toxteth, appeared after the Elementary Education Act of 1870 (see Education Offices on Sir Thomas Street), hastened by philanthropists who believed that schooling for thousands of pauper children in big cities like Liverpool was a moral obligation. Previously, education for the poor had been a voluntary affair, provided only by private individuals, religious groups, workhouses, a few specialist institutions and 'ragged' schools for young vagrants. The new law filled the gaps in the system, allowing schools (the plural use at Venice Street denotes separate classes for boys and girls) to be funded from local rates and maintained by specially-created 'boards'.

76. Liverpool Football Club, Anfield

If any institution has established the Liver Bird as an internationally recognised symbol, it is Liverpool Football Club — thanks to its unprecedented success and charismatic history in the second half of the 20th century. Its famous blue neighbours, though, have also played their part.

Wings always elevated, the bird appears in red on a white crest (1) upon the Shankly Gates (commemorating the club's legendary Scottish manager in the 60s and early 70s) at the Anfield Road end of the stadium, along with a saltire and thistle below the club anthem 'You'll Never Walk Alone'. On an adjacent set of gates the same bird is finished in gold paint (2), while at the opposite end of the ground, facing Walton Breck Road, the red Higsons Liver Bird (3) adorns the Paisley Gates that honour Shankly's successor.

The bird first appeared on the club's crest in 1901, nine years after a dispute between its founder John Houlding (a brewer, Tory politician and future mayor of the city) and the ground's original occupants, Everton FC. Formed in 1878 and originally known as St Domingo (after a local Methodist church),

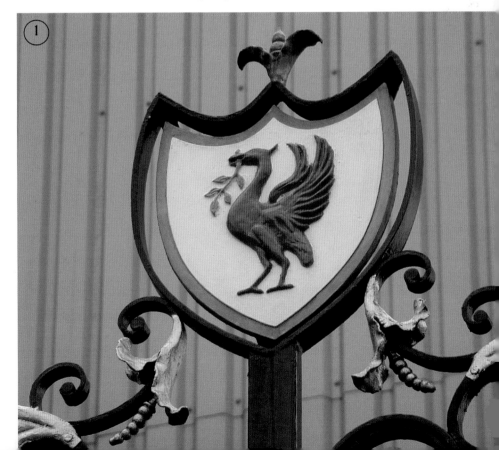

they had accepted Houlding's offer to play on a pitch at Anfield Road and use the bowls pavilion of his nearby public house, the Sandon Hotel, for dressing rooms. Interestingly, Liver Birds appear on very early Everton memorabilia.

They joined the new Football League in 1888 (Anfield was one of its inaugural grounds), won their first championship three years later but moved to a new home (Goodison) on the other side of Stanley Park when Houlding increased the rent from £100 to £250. On 15 March 1892 Houlding formed his own football club named after the city and managed by John McKenna, who would also serve as chairman. Today some of those original players and directors are buried at Anfield Cemetery. Houlding's brewery was taken over by Ind Coope & Alsop in 1938.

The name Anfield, incidentally, is a corruption of Hanging Fields, the soubriquet for the sloping farmland behind the old village of Everton.

2

77. Old Police Station, Anfield Road

In a white, oval crest stands a small Liver Bird, with a fern-like sprig in its long bill, below a crown signifying the constabulary's royal appointment. Directly above is a grinning face carved in sandstone, straight from the pages of *Alice's Adventures in Wonderland* and no doubt positioned to provide a warm welcome to the building's original guests. Standing at the corner with Harrow Road, close to Liverpool Football Club, in a district that acquired its familiar rows of terraced housing in the late 19th century, the building was most probably designed by the prolific Holme architectural practice (see the old police stations on Derby Lane in Old Swan and Lark Lane in Aigburth).

Prior to the formal establishment of Liverpool's constabulary in 1835 (see Harper Street in Kensington), the city and its environs were policed by the part-time Liverpool Night Watch. Its first superintendent was Michael James Whitty, later to become full-time chief constable before founding the *Daily Post* newspaper in 1855 (see no. 16 Wood Street). Under his supervision were 16 captains, three bridewell keepers, and 128 watchmen, patrolling 16 districts of the town. Each watchman's duties were expounded in a pamphlet printed in 1834: 'In going his rounds he will meet with many interruptions; he will be frequently called on to act, and he will have to use much firmness and great caution.

'In order that he may not act in ignorance or overstep his duty, he will, when placed on a walk, visit it frequently in the daytime and have his eyes about him at night. He will examine its different courts and alleys, acquaint himself with the names and residences of the owners of property, offices and warehouses, that he may know where to find them in the event of places being left open, or in the event of fire or robbery.

'He will also observe the persons of those who live on his walk, that he may know them if they should require his assistance; but above all, he will notice all disorderly characters and disorderly houses – first, in order to protect unsuspecting persons, and secondly, in order to prevent crime by impressing bad characters with a conviction that they are known and watched by him. In acquiring this knowledge, however, he must not enter into conversation with such people, nor enter into idle chat with any of the inhabitants. Their habits will point them out sufficiently plain, without any further enquiry...'

78. Anfield Cemetery

Two sandstone coats of arms, both in deteriorating condition, are found at the east and west entrances to one of the city's largest cemeteries, designed by Lucy & Littler (see nos. 60-62 Castle Street) in 1862 with assistance from Edward Kemp, the landscape gardener who would lay out Newsham Park six years later (see Seamen's Orphanage). A great Victorian necropolis with avenues and catacombs, it has been described as Liverpool's Pere Lachaise.

The second coat (1), on a suitably gothic clock tower with iron gates at the corner of Priory Road and Walton Lane, features Liver Birds inside and above a simple central shield, but there are two interesting deviations from the standard arms: the severely weathered, conch-blowing triton faces inwards (perhaps a call to the earth rather than, traditionally, the sea) and there is a human skull at the feet of the seated Neptune. A relief of a more elegant and intact Liver Bird (2) appears on the exterior of the nearby sexton's lodge.

On the coat above the eastern Cherry Lane entrance in Walton, a long-necked Liver Bird (3) occupies a central shield, flanked by curious, winged gargoyles (one of which has been decapitated). Like an ancient ruin, the entire relief is overgrown with vegetation and both the Neptune's trident and triton's right hand are missing. Another Liver Bird (4), in equally poor condition, stands in an adjacent crest topped with a shell.

Inside the cemetery, local sculptor Herbert Tyson Smith's city coat of arms (see the Cenotaph on St George's Plateau) appears upon the May Blitz Memorial (5). Unveiled in 1951, it marks a 170ft long communal grave for

554 victims (373 unidentified) of the most intense period of bombing raids upon Merseyside during World War Two. In May 1941 alone, sirens sounded 509 times. Symbols of faith are absent from the memorial because the grave contains persons of unknown nationality and religion.

Among others buried in the cemetery: Daniel Higson (died 1914), founder of Liverpool's foremost brewery; Michael J. Whitty (1873), the town's first head constable and inaugural editor of the *Liverpool Daily Post*; James Mace (1910), heavyweight bareknuckle champion of the world; John Dermott (1895), one of the original directors of Liverpool Football Club; Thomas A. Bradshaw (1899), Liverpool FC player and England international; William Young (1866), soldier at Waterloo;

Reginald M. Makepeace MC (1918), World War One flying ace; Douglas Pomford (1960), SAS; William Tomkinson (1897), builder of the Lewis's store on Ranelagh Street; T.J. Hughes (1933), founder of the eponymously-named shop on London Road; Captain John Chadwick (1869), Balaclava hero; Sir John Utting (1927), surgeon; Robert S.B. Leech (1881), captain in the 24th Regiment, Zulu Wars; Robert A. Smythe (1920), hero of Rorke's Drift; William Patrick Mylotte (1870), Victoria Cross, Indian Mutiny; Leonard Noblett (1911), owner of toffee shops; and James Maybrick (1889), whose wife Florence was acquitted on appeal of poisoning him with arsenic in one of Liverpool's most famous murder trials (see the Old Police Station on Lark Lane).

3

79. Alsop High School, Delf Lane

A stone coat of arms in excellent condition above the entrance to this erstwhile boys comprehensive school, now a technology college, opposite Walton Hall Park close to Queens Drive's intersection with Rice Lane. With its conspicuously webbed feet, crestless head and apparent lack of a tail, the bird in the central shield is a dead ringer for a mallard or shoveler duck of heraldic legend.

80. Old Bank, 475 Queens Drive

A gilded Liver Bird in a simple laurel surmounts the entrance to this building — almost certainly a former bank, probably a suburban branch of Martins — at the broad, majestic boulevard's junction with Townsend Lane, where West Derby, Anfield and Norris Green meet.

Begun in 1904, over six miles in length and linking all of Liverpool's radial arterial routes (from Rice Lane in Walton to Smithdown Road in Wavertree), Queens Drive was the pièce de résistance of John Brodie, latterly one of the chief engineers of the Queensway Tunnel and responsible for the widening of several major streets in the city centre. As an undertaking, it resonated with similar grand projects in America — at roughly the same time, Chicago's own great urban planner Daniel Burnham published plans for a grand circulatory thoroughfare connecting the main roads emanating from his own city's Lake Michigan waterfront.

81. Barclays Bank, Mill Lane, West Derby Village

The same bird and laurel as no. 475 Queens Drive, this time worked in stone and inside the pediment of another cornerside bank building, here at the junction with Eaton Road in West Derby Village. Other architectural similarities include the twin pilasters, central acroterion (classical shell-like decoration) above the entrance and circular projecting skylight on the roof.

West Derby is far older than Liverpool (see Brougham Terrace) with an entry in the Domesday Book for its royal hunting forest. But today's village was remodelled by the Molyneux family, Earls of Sefton, in the 1850s to complement their ancestral home at nearby Croxteth Hall (fellow aristocrats the Stanleys, Earls of Derby, were based at Knowsley Hall). A new parish church and village square, along with dozens of mansions owned by Liverpool 'merchant princes' like the Tates and Holts, were added to a medieval courthouse and yeoman's house. The abundance of sandstone buildings and greenery preserve the village's rustic feel.

82. Melwood, West Derby

On the frosted glass entrance to Liverpool FC's training complex, off Melwood Drive in suburban West Derby, is the biggest representation of a Liver Bird after those on the Royal Liver Building, based upon the club's traditional and world-famous emblem.

The design was part of a £3 million, purpose-built upgrade of the football club's renowned training base in 2002, providing state-of-the-art facilities for the first-team squad and backroom staff, and featuring new dressing rooms, synthetic pitches, treatment rooms, saunas, gynmasium, restaurant and media facilities. The main building's official title is the Millennium Pavilion.

83. Old Police Station, Derby Lane, Old Swan

The same Liver Bird and crest from the police station on Anfield Road is repeated in the pediment of this building, since converted into a probation office, but here the crown is set off with a tiny, gargoylesque face and either side are collared 'talbots' (bloodhounds) 'environed' (surrounded) by Lancashire roses and holding feathered quills decorated with fleurs-de-lys in their forepaws.

Traditionally, dogs denote vigilance and loyalty and feathers are symbols of obedience, and here they have further heraldic connotations. During the reign of Charles I (1625-49), the Talbots were a powerful Liverpool family who left their mark in the name of several taverns in the city (there was a famous Talbot Arms on Water Street, for instance). The quills also represent St John the Evangelist, patron saint of both writers and King John, whose son granted Liverpool its charter and seal, while the fleurs-de-lys are derived from the arms of Thomas, Earl of Lancaster.

Together, the dogs and feathers symbolise not the modern city of Liverpool but the medieval West Derby Hundred (see Brougham Terrace) of the county of Lancaster, whose old crest they support above the grand entrance of County Sessions House on William Brown Street. Completed in 1884, the latter building was designed by George G. Holme and Francis Usher Holme (see their Conservative Club/Municipal Annexe and Hahnemann Hospital), a duo that also worked upon several police stations in the region – one of which was probably this outpost on Derby Lane.

Still with heraldry, Old Swan takes its name from the district's Three Swans public house, which in turn recognised the arms of the Walton family that once owned land in the area.

84. Old Bank, 611 West Derby Road, Tuebrook

A sculpture 'in the round' of a powerfully-built Liver Bird with inflated breast and thorn-like crest stands guard between carved swags and ribbons above this former suburban branch of Martins Bank (now occupied by a deli) straddling two roads. Its sharp beak and half-spread wings are reminiscent of the eagle of Barclays Bank (which took over Martins in 1969), but the webbed feet and attendant seaweed confirm its true identity. Compare its front-facing aspect to the bird on the former fire station on Kirkdale's Westminster Road.

Tuebrook, named after an ancient stream and situated between Anfield and Newsham Park, was transformed from rural hamlet to urban village by the Victorians, with small businesses and banks cramming its main thoroughfare. Surviving Martins branches are characterised by both their decorative sculpture and classical architectural solidity. This building was erected around 1910, eight years before the merger with the long-established Bank of Liverpool that made Martins a major player on the national financial scene.

85. Seamen's Orphanage, Newsham Park

A Liver Bird with cotton-wool plumage (1) stands in a simple hanging shield carved upon the corner tower of this former orphanage, opened in 1876 in the grounds of Liverpool's first truly public park. In the pediment above the adjacent entrance is a sailing ship with a Liver Bird on an ensign (2) at its stern.

All Gothic Revival style and red-brick-and-terracotta substance, this building and the North Western Hotel on Lime Street are architect Alfred Waterhouse's earliest gifts to his native city (see his later Victoria Building and Royal Infirmary). By then he had already received the Grand Prize for Architecture in Paris, and two years after the orphanage's completion he became an associate member of the Royal Academy of Arts and received a gold medal from the Royal Institute of British Architects.

Newsham Park had been laid out in 1868 by Edward Kemp, author of the seminal landscaping book *How To Lay Out A Small Garden*, co-architect of the earlier Birkenhead Park, and one of the judges in New York's Central Park competition. The first of Liverpool's trio of great parks (flanked by Stanley to the north-east and Sefton to the south-east), it featured an aviary, band stand, boating lake, fishing lake and five fountains, and adjoined an earlier mansion house occupied by Queen Victoria in 1886 when she attended an International Exhibition of Navigation, Commerce and Industry at Edge Hill. Another notable visitor was William F. Cody, better known as Buffalo Bill, who brought his Wild West Show here in 1891.

86. The Belmont, 303 West Derby Road, Anfield

Within walking distance of Liverpool FC's stadium is a suitably red, stone Liver Bird, almost 'in the round' upon a white-tile background in the pediment of this grand, port-holed public house, dating from 1885, at the crossroads with Belmont Road and Sheil Road near to Newsham Park. The bird's dramatic location, vivid colour and size – note the long neck and top-heavy head – belies its somewhat shabby condition close up. Aside from its footballing heritage (inside the pub, miscellaneous Liverpool FC memorabilia adorns the walls of the bar), Belmont Road was famous for its old workhouse that became Newsham General Hospital, and a landmark Welsh Presbyterian Church.

87. Ogden's, Boundary Lane, Kensington

The motif of this historic Liverpool company
– as famous for its cards and coupons as its
cigarettes – is a white, dove-like Liver Bird
with a short neck, small bill, and wings raised
as it perches upon a tobacco oast (kiln for
storing and curing leaves) with a castle turret
above its raised head. It appears as a mosaic
(1) upon the vestibule floor of this grandiose
red-brick and white-stone factory, and in a
sculpted relief secured by serene cherubs
(2) above the main entrance.

Liverpool imported and stored vast
quantities of raw tobacco from the Carolinas,

Virginia, Kentucky and Tennessee in the 19th century, and Thomas Ogden opened his first shop on Park Road in 1860. A decade later he ran a factory and snuff mill on St James Street, then Cornwallis Street, before the business moved to this site off West Derby Road in 1899.

At its height, Ogden's employed 4,000 workers and produced 40 million cigarettes per week from a room one-third of a mile in length. Every year it manufactured a total length of 'twist' or spun tobacco five times the distance between Liverpool and New York. Among its most famous brands was St Bruno pipe tobacco, launched in 1896.

Following Ogden's hostile takeover by the American Tobacco Company in 1901 — when tobacco tycoon James Buchanan Duke walked into the factory and bought it on the spot — a dozen other British firms formed the Imperial Tobacco Company. After a subsequent trade war Ogden's was surrendered to Imperial, who abandoned plans to enter the American market and founded the British American Tobacco Company in 1902.

Up to the outbreak of World War Two, Ogden's also produced coupons exchangeable for prizes and sets of collectable illustrated cigarette cards or 'stiffeners' (their original function was to strengthen the flimsy packaging) with themes ranging from 'Football Club Colours' and 'Australian Test Cricketers' to 'Flags & Funnels of Leading Steamship Lines' and 'Picturesque People of the Empire'. The cards were a guaranteed craze among young boys who begged, stole or borrowed them from adults and swapped them with friends.

88. Brougham Terrace, West Derby Road

Change here for the origins of Liverpool's most famous hospitals and the country's first-ever mosque. In the foyer of this once elegant but now rather forsaken Georgian terrace is a Liver Bird, carved in wood and encircled by the words 'The Select Vestry of the Parish of Liverpool' as part of a commemoration of the West Derby Union from the turn of the last century. Until recently, the building housed the local Registry for Births, Deaths & Marriages.

Created in 1699, the parish of Liverpool was responsible for administrating the Elizabethan Poor Laws to relieve the destitute. Records from the Liverpool Town Books of 1648 show that displaced 'yong Children and

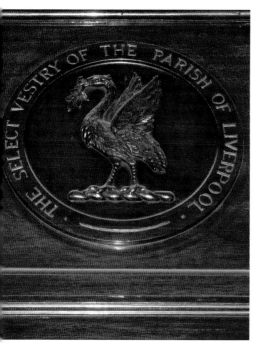

Beggars wch...are found Wandring and begging contrarie to Lawe' were to be 'shipt for the Barbadoes or otherwise to be put apprentices if ye belong to this Towne'.

In 1922 its jurisdiction passed to the West Derby Union, which since 1837 had comprised 23 local parishes (not including Liverpool to the west or Prescot to the east) and presided over the construction of several institutes for the poor: the Walton Workhouse (1869) that eventually became Walton Hospital; the Belmont Road Institution (1890) that evolved into Newsham General; and a further site in West Derby (1906) 'for the accommodation of chronic infirm paupers' that is now Alder Hey.

Named after Liverpool lawyer and Whig politician Henry Peter, 1st Baron of Brougham and Vaux, the terrace was designed in 1830 by James A. Picton (see his later Union Marine Buildings at 11 Dale Street). The West Derby Union moved into nos. 1-7 in 1900, but 11 years earlier nos. 8-10 had been opened as the Liverpool Muslim Institute by William Abdullah Quilliam, the son of a wealthy watch manufacturer (and also descendant of the first lieutenant on HMS *Victory*) who at 17 had been sent to Morocco to recuperate from illness and subsequently converted to Islam.

On 18 April 1891, the city's first Muslim funeral was reported by the *Liverpool Review* thus: 'It looked rather strange to see the member of the congregation who officiated as Imam clad in a suit of light tweed, and for the presiding Mullah to be attired in a light blue tie and kid gloves'.

When Quilliam moved to Turkey in 1908, his Muslim community dissolved and many members moved to England's first purpose-built mosque in Woking.

89. Old Bridewell, Harper Street, Kensington

A weathered coat of arms above a former police station and bridewell off Prescot Street, near to the Royal Liverpool University Hospital, and similar to the arms on the Blue Coat School on Wavertree's Church Road. Here, parts of the original red sandstone are still visible between layers of soot.

The Liver Bird in the central crest also resembles that on the Cunard Building on the Pier Head while the upper bird, its caricatured head too large for its body, rises above the building's parapet within a shell.

The origins of Liverpool's constabulary lie in local elections of 1835 when the victorious Whigs instituted Robert Peel's recommendations (in 1829 he had founded the Metropolitan Police). The town's first head constable was Michael James Whitty, later to found the *Liverpool Daily Post* newspaper (see no. 16 Wood Street). At his disposal were 290 men, 24 inspectors, four superintendents, and 40 bridewell keepers and office workers. Upon retiring from the service in 1844 he was presented with 1,000 guineas by his staff 'in remembrance of his gentlemanly conduct'. Sixteen years later, frequent visitor Charles Dickens noted that Liverpool's force was 'much better than the metropolitan system... in all respects it tempers its remarkable vigilance with a still more remarkable discretion'.

90. Old Bank, Deane Road, Kensington

Two fierce birds with curved beaks stand in heraldic shields high up in arched recesses upon the adjoining façades of this former branch of Martins Bank, at the corner of Deane Road and Kensington Street.

The building was erected in 1898, but above both shields is the date 1831 – possibly a reference to the year in which the Bank of Liverpool, acquired much later by Martins, was originally founded. The accompanying shell motifs and ornate decoration are certainly reminiscent of the Bank of Liverpool's erstwhile headquarters at no. 45 Victoria Street.

Liverpool branches of Martins are invariably grand designs, more landmarks than mere banks, and this branch has been attributed to Scottish architect James Robert Rhind, who was noted for his flamboyant style and designed seven of Glasgow's Carnegie libraries in the very early 1900s. With its miniature columns and undulating blend of concave and convex elements, the building moved Liverpool architectural historian Quentin Hughes to recall the Church of San Carlo alle Quattro Fontane in Rome – a 17th century Baroque masterpiece.

By the time this branch opened, Kensington had grown from stagecoach route between Old Swan and Prescot into a warren of red-brick terrace housing, with several streets named after Queen Victoria's German in-laws (Leopold, Bathenburg, Guelph, Albert and Adelaide). A few yards south along Deane Road is one of Liverpool's lost Jewish cemeteries, opened in 1837 but derelict for a century.

91. Grosvenor Hotel, Lodge Lane

A pair of swan-like Liver Birds click beaks in an arcane courtship ritual in a relief panel on this former public house at the corner with Ritson Street. It was erected in 1884, two years before Queen Victoria passed along the lane in an open carriage while visiting the International Exhibition of Navigation, Commerce & Industry at Edge Hill (see Park Hospital in Newsham Park).

The 1880s brought Lodge Lane's late transformation from semi-rural retreat to high-density housing. Its name recalls the two high-gated lodges — one at the thoroughfare's present junction with Smithdown Road and the other in Dingle — that marked the old boundary wall of the Royal & Ancient Park of Toxteth.

Liverpool's original Renaissance man, William Roscoe, died at his cottage here in 1831, having moved from his previous home at Allerton Hall (and before that, addresses in Islington and Dingle) and 50 years later a large Wesleyan church (since demolished) was built in the vicinity. In the 1930s, the lane had a barber shop run by Jack Robinson, the country's foremost musical-saw entertainer, and an upholsterer's business owned by singer Frankie Vaughan's father. Today, it is one of Liverpool's most multi-cultural communities.

92. Granby Street Board Schools, Toxteth

Another school for poor children founded after the passing of the 1870 Elementary Education Act. Built in 1880, six years before its northern equivalent on Venice Street in Anfield, it is crowned by a semi-circular pediment with a brick-lined porthole. Inside, a smooth-headed Liver Bird holding a three-leafed sprig of seaweed stands in bulrushes – a motif found elsewhere (see nos. 34-48 London Road) and here perhaps alluding to the Moses fable. Entrances for girls and infants explain the use of 'schools' in the plural.

Post-war Granby Street began to acquire its cosmopolitan character when Liverpool's resident black population, mostly ex-seamen from as far afield as Sierra Leone and Surinam, moved here from the bombed Pitt Street area and helped to establish a legendary club scene – its new and exciting music contributing towards Liverpool's beat explosion in the late 1950s and early 1960s. A small group of Indians also settled in Toxteth following the country's independence in 1947, and Granby's most recent influx has brought Somalis fleeing civil war in the early 1990s.

93. Princes Boulevard, Toxteth

Colletively, a boulevard as aesthetic in conception as any in Europe. Technically, a parallel-running road and avenue separated by a central tree-lined promenade and linking Georgian Liverpool with Princes Park. Halfway along, this pair of Liver Birds with classic tea-spout necks adorn a flamboyant, fluted lamp standard surmounting a drinking fountain.

The 1902 *New Illustrated Guide to Liverpool* noted that 'from end to end are seen churches of all denominations'. Among them, the fabulous Old Hebrew Congregation Synagogue (now Grade II listed), exotic Greek Orthodox Church of St Nicholas (still in use) and imposing Welsh Presbyterian Church (under renovation).

The thoroughfare may have been a Victorian perambulator's paradise, but an exposé in a January 1877 edition of *The Liverpool Critic* detected a less reputable aspect to its character at night, when it became 'an unlicensed place of public amusement' notorious for 'the loud-toned behaviour of the juvenile snob upon whose lip is flourishing the first bloom of an early down, and from between whose teeth — as he stalks majestically down Princes Road, tipping the wink to this girl and tossing a knowing nod to that other — are languidly emitted the volcanic puffs from a first new meerschaum [pipe]...

'It is not a crime to be a shop-girl, but — be it confessed — shop-girls of the kind that frequent Princes Road are in the main vain, foolish, childish, extravagantly fond of dress and, generally, of a disposition in every respect fitted for the inroads of wealthy depravity...

'A terribly insidious influence is exercised upon vain little butterflies by the familiar attentions of those fellows of higher rank who prowl about this district. When a man manifestly escapes from his own social circle to introduce himself to a girl of humbler means, he often provokes the suspicion that under the cover of his anonymity and by the strength of his purse he contemplates an illicit intrigue. This is an assumption which — relative to the frequenters of Princes Road — I can adduce the most pitiable facts to substantiate.'

94. High Park Street reservoir, Dingle

A sandstone Liver Bird with cocked wings, duck's bill and tiny puncture for an eye is carved upon a solid block of this Victorian service reservoir's 4ft thick wall, located in one of the highest parts of town – ensuring that water could flow downhill under gravity to save the cost of pumping. Today, this hulking, utilitarian structure houses a local community centre, but its existence symbolises a controversial chapter in Liverpool history and the re-awakening of Welsh nationalism.

Designed in 1853 by Thomas Duncan, waterworks engineer to the Corporation, the reservoir originally received supplies from Rivington on the western flank of the Pennines, 25 miles to the north-east (six years earlier, an act had been passed allowing Liverpool to seek water outside its city limits). But Liverpool's exponential growth soon outstripped supply, and in 1866 Duncan explored the Lake District, Pennines and Wales for a further source of water that could satisfy one million people in the city and its suburbs.

In 1879 his successor George Deacon proposed the building of a huge masonry dam along a river valley at Vyrnwy in mid-Wales, 70 miles from Liverpool, that necessitated the drowning of a village called Llanwddyn (whose ruins can still be seen when water levels drop in dry summers).

Upon the dam's completion a decade later, the *Illustrated London News* described it as 'one of the grandest engineering works of modern times', 100ft high and 1,172ft long, with a newly-created lake able to supply 40 million gallons daily. Its aqueduct consisted of two cast-iron pipes passing through several tunnels and three feeder reservoirs before it reached Prescot, from whence water was distributed to High Park Street and Margaret Street in Everton (also desiged by Duncan).

Barely 65 years later the Corporation of Liverpool won government permission to build a new reservoir in the Tryweryn valley, north of Bala, drowning another village (Capel Celyn) in the process. Despite fierce protests by local residents and politicians, the dam was completed in 1965. A year later, Plaid Cymru won its first seat in parliament, and more recently Liverpool City Council issued a formal apology.

95. Old Bank, 147 Park Road, Toxteth

A small but fierce-looking Liver Bird stands within the pediment above the entrance of the former 'south branch' of the Liverpool Savings Bank, which, like the Liverpool Union Bank (see Halifax House on Fenwick Street), latterly became part of what is now Lloyds TSB. Erected in 1882, the branch was designed by Grayson & Ould, the architectural duo behind many fine financial buildings in the city centre (see Victoria Chambers on Castle Street).

It once served a thriving community on a smart thoroughfare crammed with shops and small businesses, scored by tramlines, and close to churches, boys clubs and public baths. Running parallel here with Princes Boulevard to the north, Park Road once extended from the junction of Great George Street and Parliament Street through the Dingle and right along Aigburth Road (as it was renamed in 1837) to the southern fringes of Sefton Park – all originally part of the Royal & Ancient Park of Toxteth.

Near its highest point is the High Park Street reservoir and the adjacent 'Welsh streets' – a series of Victorian terraced rows built and largely occcupied by Welsh immigrants, who also worked on Liverpool's docks (see nos. 60-62 Castle Street). One of them, Madryn Street, was the childhood home of Beatles drummer Ringo Starr. Appropriately, back on Park Road – and near to the 'Holy Land' quartet of streets called David, Isaac, Jacob and Moses and first settled by Puritan families from the Midlands at the start of the 17th century – there are views across the river and Wirral peninsula to the North Welsh hills. Back towards town, on the opposite side of the road, are more themed streets, this time named after Charles Dickens novels (Dombey, Pickwick, Dorrit).

96. Brunswick Station, Sefton Street

The crest of Liverpool City Engineers – the same Liver Bird from Leigh, Boundary Street and Sandhills Bridges – appears here upon two plaques from 1866 commemorating the erection of a bridge serving the Brunswick railway station. Opened two years earlier, the original station was the terminus of the Garston & Liverpool Railway Line. It closed in 1874 when the line was diverted to Liverpool Central but re-opened in 1998 as a stop between Hunts Cross, the city centre and Southport on the Northern Line of the Merseyrail suburban system.

Opposite is Brunswick Dock, the first to be built by Jesse Hartley (see Sherlocks Bar on Regent Road) when he became the city's dock engineer in 1824. Opened eight years later, it was dominated by first the timber trade (from Baltic and Canadian ports) then grain imports until 1975, when cargoes were discharged by bulk carriers at Seaforth's modern terminal.

97. Toxteth Annexe, Aigburth Road

A terracotta coat of arms, a century old and in good nick, lies in the pediment above the entrance to the former Toxteth Technical College (now a training centre) near Dingle Vale. The squat, fowl-like Liver Bird in the central shield bears some resemblance to the bird on the façade of the Cunard Building on the Pier Head.

A foundation stone in the foyer marks the school's opening in 1907. It provided two years of study for 150 boys aged between 13 and 15, who could 'produce a declaration from their parents or guardians that it is their intention to keep them at the school for the full course, and to send them on to some trade or industrial occupation'. An 'admission fee' of 15 shillings per term was required, and there were 15 scholarships available.

Minutes from a Liverpool Education Committee meeting in June 1908 suggested the following curriculum: Elementery Science, Practical Mathematics, Geometry and Practical Drawing, Freehand Drawing and Sketching, Handwork in Wood and Metal, Physical Exercises, English Composition and Literature, and Geography of Products, Manufacture and Transport.

98. Old Bank, 301 Aigburth Road, Aigburth

Another former branch of Martins Bank, another Liver Bird. Here it is carved in low relief within a cartouche above the entrance to a large, green-turreted building (now a bar) dating from the turn of the last century and straddling the corner with Ashfield Road. Tall and proud with raised wings, it bears more resemblance to the birds on the former Martins branch on Kensington's Deane Road than those on the bank's headquarters on Water Street or its outposts along Queens Drive.

Aigburth means 'place of the oak trees' in Anglo-Saxon, and its leafy character was retained by affluent Victorian merchants who built many villas set within large private gardens in the area. The bank stands at the point where its semi-rustic charm blends gently into Grassendale's sedate 1930s suburbia.

99. Sefton Park, Aigburth

Liver Birds appear on two of the six entrances to this magnificent Victorian park, one of the city's great green lungs. Weathered coats of arms (I) are carved upon either side on the monumental gates at the slip road connecting Aigburth Road and Aigburth Drive, while two sculpted birds (2) project from the grand arched entrance at the junction of Aigburth Drive and Ullet Road.

This latter pair are so plausibly proportioned – wader's legs and webbed feet, hunched V-shaped wings and slender S-shaped necks (one sadly amputated), and fish rather than seaweed in their short, concave bills – they could be based upon a true species found in the park's lake and woodland. As it is, herons and crested grebes are frequently sighted in the park, along with swans, geese and the occasional cormorant. At 200 acres,

it remains a haven for wildlife over 130 years after it was opened to the public.

Originally open countryside, then part of the Royal & Ancient Park of Toxteth, the land was acquired by Sir Richard Molyneux of Sefton at the start of the 17th century and purchased by the Corporation of Liverpool in 1864. Local architect Louis Hornblower and Edouard André, a Parisian pupil of Napoleon III's gardener, won a competition to design the new park, their winning entry a fairytale landscape of winding pathways, statues and grottos, and streams with cascades, stepping stones and bridges. In 1872 it was officially opened by Prince Arthur, third son of Queen Victoria (who paid her own visit 14 years later). Enclosing the park was a ring of large, private houses — many of whose entrance gates featured locks embossed with Liver Birds and the inscription Sefton Park 1871 — punctuated by Hansel and Gretel keepers' lodges. The famous Palm House, now fully restored and Grade II listed, was added in 1896.

100. Old Police Station, Lark Lane, Aigburth

Two small Liver Birds appear upon the façade of this former police station on Aigburth's quaintly-named, bohemian enclave – one with wings raised between a pair of red Lancashire roses in a rectangular relief panel (1), the other less agitated upon a simple crest in a square niche (2).

The building was designed in 1885 by Francis Usher Hulme in collaboration with his uncle, George G. Holme. Four years later, it welcomed its most celebrated guest in Florence Maybrick, accused of poisoning her husband James with arsenic and subsequently sentenced to death in a case that still fascinates criminologists.

A 'Southern Belle' from Alabama, she had married James Maybrick, a Liverpool cotton broker 24 years her senior, after a whirlwind romance aboard the SS *Baltic* bound for Paris. By the time the couple settled in an Aigburth mansion, Maybrick had become a clandestine 'arsenic eater' – addicted to the substance after taking it to combat malaria during a previous visit to the United States – while also keeping a secret mistress in London's Whitechapel.

Upon her husband's death from 'inflammation of the stomach and bowels' in May 1889 Florence was arrested, held initially at Aigburth police station and summoned via Walton Gaol to the Assizes Court at St George's Hall in a week-long trial, littered with suspicion, rumour and innuendo that thrilled Britain and America. After 35 minutes the jury found her guilty of murder, but just four days before she was due to hang the verdict was overturned by the Home Secretary and the sentence commuted to life imprisonment. Fifteen years later, Florence was released. She returned to America, died a recluse in 1941 and was buried in Connecticut. Her husband's body lies in Anfield Cemetery.

In 1993 the case acquired a sensational new dimension when a diary, purportedly written by James Maybrick, was discovered in Liverpool. Among its entries were graphic descriptions of murders committed in Whitechapel, the year before Maybrick's death, by Jack the Ripper. Its authenticity is debated to this day.

101. Unitarian Church, Ullet Road, Aigburth

Two Liver Birds with the distinctive shape and glossy-black plumage of a cormorant appear in a stained-glass coat of arms at this historic and artistically significant church. Below the arms is an Arthurian representation of Sir Sydney Jones, wartime mayor of Liverpool, his title signified by the knight's helmet upon which the upper bird perches (similar helmets are found in the arms on the ceiling of St George's Hall and the stained-glass blazonry of the Mersey Docks & Harbour Company in the Port of Liverpool Building). The window was executed by William Wilson of Edinburgh, one of the country's foremost stained-glass makers, whose windows appear in some of Scotland's most famous churches.

Jones was a latterday member of a Unitarian congregation with a strong tradition in the city (see Central Hall). Dominated by Liverpool's free-thinking merchant class from the 19th century – including famous local families like the Rathbones, Holts and Roscoes – it challenged orthodox theology and was characterised by powerful preaching and intellectual stimulation. Among its national adherents was Joseph Priestley, the discoverer of oxygen, who eventually became a Unitarian minister.

The church was built in 1899 close to Sefton Park, itself opened for just 27 years. Now Grade I listed, it also features windows designed by the Pre-Raphaelite artist Edward Burne-Jones and fashioned in the William Morris workshop between 1901 and 1928, along with murals by Portuguese symbolist Gerald Moira, who decorated one of London's most famous churches, All Saints.

102. Picton Road Baths, Wavertree

A whole legion of handsome Liver Birds, made from glazed ceramic tiles, live along a corridor inside these fomer public baths opened in 1906 and since converted into council offices adjacent to Wavertree Library. Suitably sea green, they stand inside crests decorated with swags and foliage on top of pilasters punctuating decorative friezes along the walls, but curiously in their bills they hold flower buds instead of seaweed.

These were one of a dozen baths, often accompanied by laundries and wash houses, built in Liverpool between 1851 and 1923, following the establishment of a Baths Committee to oversee their management. Other venues included Cornwallis Street, Steble Street, Westminster Road, Lodge Lane, Lister Drive, Queens Drive, Stanley Park and Burlington Street. Mixed-sex bathing, however, was not permitted until 1914. Picton Road Baths celebrated their centenary in 2006 with a new 50-metre, Olympic-standard swimming pool earmarked for the site.

103. Blue Coat School, Church Road, Wavertree

The Liverpool coat of arms sits in a recess above the doorway to one of the city's most historic schools, withdrawn from School Lane (see Bluecoat Chambers) to what was rural Wavertree in 1906. The entrance's arrangement of triangular pediment, arched bay and Ionic columns — as well as the dome of the school's chapel — is typical of architects Thornley, Briggs and Wolstenholme, who designed the baroque Port of Liverpool Building at the same time.

Co-founded at the beginning of the 18th century by rector Robert Styth and slave trader, master mariner and future mayor Bryan Blundell (after whom the street near Queens Dock is named), the school was originally a 'foundling hospital' for orphans of sailors lost at sea. Its name derives from the blue frock coats (the colour of alms-giving and charity) worn here and at similar schools like Christ's Hospital in London as an indicator of poverty. As late as 1948 it switched from orphanage to secondary day school for boys only, by which time the disinctive uniform was phased out.

104. War Memorial, Holy Trinity Church, Wavertree

There is a touch of poignancy about the Liver Bird carved in relief upon this monolithic sandstone cross, dating from 1920, in the parish churchyard adjacent to the Blue Coat School. Upon the memorial's western face is the inscription 'To the enduring memory of the Wavertree men who laid down their lives in the Great War.' On the opposite side, the bird's long-billed head is lowered, its wings are raised but not extended, and twin fronds of seaweed have been released from its beak to rest solemnly upon the waves beneath. Above and below are the words '1914-1919 Pro Patria 1939-1945'.

The monument's tall, tapered shape and the female figures on its narrower north and south elevations are reminiscent of the war memorial at Birkenhead's Hamilton Square, completed five years later. Both the latter structure and the Cenotaph on St George's Plateau were the work of sculptor Herbert Tyson Smith and architect Lionel Budden, who would eventually replace the charismatic Charles Reilly as the head of the University's School of Architecture & Applied Arts. A fair assumption that this, too, is their creation. Ten years before the monument's erection, Reilly himself was commissioned to remodel the church interior to cope with the parish's growing congregation. The original building was completed in 1794.

105. Calderstones Park, Allerton

Two silver Liver Birds, their shaggy feathers, sharp beaks and rigid posture lending them the air of cockerels, occupy ornate badges on the park's massive wrought-iron entrance gates at the corner of Calderstones Road and Harthill Road. The theatrical aspect is completed by Atlantes — carvings of the Titan in Greek mythology who held up the pillars of the universe — upon each gate pier. Here, like Hercules, they wear lion skins with the paws tied across the waist. Originally, they stood guard outside a city centre office building designed by James Picton (see his Union Marine Buildings on Dale Street) and next to the Town Hall.

A century old in 2005, Calderstones was created when 126 acres of parkland were sold to the Corporation by the MacIver shipping family, whose patriarch Charles MacIver had originally established the British & North American Royal Steam Packet Company with Samuel Cunard. Named after a stone formation dating back 4,000 years, the park was augmented by the 32-acre Harthill estate during World War One and became the most recent home to Liverpool's historic Botanic Garden founded by William Roscoe (see nos. 34-36 Castle Street). Like Sefton Park, it has its own lake and glasshouse, plus ornamental gardens, exotic plant collection and ancient oak tree.

106. Gateacre Fountain, Grange Lane, Gateacre

A Liver Bird in a crest wreathed by swirling seaweed occupies one side of this hexagonal sandstone gazebo, originally housing a drinking fountain and erected, reads its inscription, 'by the people of Gateacre in memory of John H. Wilson, 1883'. Griffons, gargoyles and twin-tailed mermaids, bashing cymbals and blowing horns, add to the decoration.

John Hays Wilson was chairman of Liverpool's Water Committee when it proposed the building of a dam at Vyrnwy, in mid-Wales, to supply the town with water (see High Park Street in Dingle). He died before its completion and the land for his memorial was donated by another distinguished resident of this rustic southern suburb – Andrew Barclay Walker, a former mayor of Liverpool who had paid for the construction of the eponymously-named art gallery on William Brown Street a decade earlier.

107. Birkenhead Brewery, Woodside

Look over the water for a rare sighting of Liverpool's emblem in the livery of the now defunct Birkenhead Brewery. In a niche on the façade of the former Pier Head Hotel, at the corner of Hamilton Square facing Woodside, a gilded Liver Bird (1) with magnificent wings perches upon a barrel above a crest consisting of a buckled belt, featuring the brewery's name and a jade-green shield bearing the legend Peerless Ales & Stout. A red bird (2) appears in the same motif above the entrance to the Lord Raglan Hotel (named after a veteran of Waterloo and the Crimea) roughly a mile away at the corner of New Chester Road and Union Street in Tranmere.

The brewery was founded on Oxton Road when two existing businesses, Aspinalls and Cooks, amalgamated in 1865. Almost a century later it was taken over by Threlfall Chesters Brewers, itself absorbed by Whitbread in 1967. Public houses like the Pier Head and Lord Raglan served a local population that had swelled from the early 19th century – first with the founding of the Cammel Laird shipbuilding dynasty in 1824, then with the supervision of Birkenhead's docks by the Mersey Docks & Harbour Company in 1857 and their expansion by the son of the great engineer Jesse Hartley (see Sherlocks Bar on Regent Road, Vauxhall).

By then, the beautiful stone-faced buildings of Hamilton Square were rivalling those of Edinburgh, and Birkenhead Park – designed by Sir Joseph Paxton and Edward Kemp (see Park Hospital, Newsham Park) – had become a fabulous template for Central Park in New York.

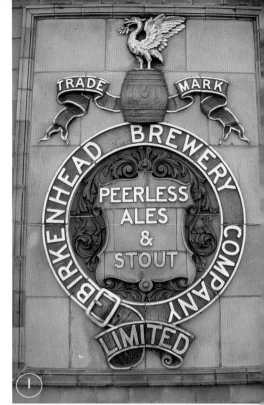

108. Old Bank, 72 King Street, Wallasey

There is almost a touch of hieroglyphics about this severely-weathered Liver Bird, its legs worn away by the passage of time and impact of the elements, but its pictographic wings, head and sprig of seaweed still visible.

It stands in a cartouche within a broken pediment above the entrance to this former bank building on King Street, part of the long thoroughfare that links New Brighton to Birkenhead. Wallasey owes its urban landscape to the opening of the Queensway Tunnel in 1934, after which the townships of Liscard, Seacombe, Egremont, New Brighton, Wallasey Village, Poulton and Leasowe gradually merged. Its borough coat of arms features a ship, dolphin and trident, indicating Wallasey's maritime heritage and medieval status as an embarkation point to rival Liverpool.

Previous pages miscellany: Davies Publicity, Clifford Stree; bollard, Exchange Flags; Central Library glass; Linacre Hotel, Bootle; Liver Launderette, Allerton; St Petersburg restaurant, York Street; Mather Avenue fire station, Allerton; advertising hoarding, Scotland Road; Victoria Courtyard, University; lamp standard, William Brown Street; Students Union, University; JMU Avril Robarts Centre, Tithebarn Street; Liverpool FC store, Williamson Square; Daily Post & Echo, Old Hall Street; public bin, Dale Street; Colin's Bridewell, Campbell Square; advertising hoarding, Hall Lane; Heritage Walk paving, Water Street; Liverpool Film Studios, Kirkdale; Liverpool Direct gates, East Prescot Road; public toilet, Bold Street; Park Lodge gates, Sefton Park Road; Hilllsborough Memorial tapestry, Millennium House; heritage signpost, Strand

SELECT BIBLIOGRAPHY

Absolute Integrity: The Story of Royal Insurance 1845-1995, Peter Pugh (Cambridge Business Publishing, 1995).

A Pub On Every Corner, Volume One: Liverpool City Centre, Freddy O'Connor (Bluecoat Press, 1995).

Armorial Bearings of the City of Liverpool, John Paul Rylands (paper read before Historic Society of Lancashire & Cheshire, printed by Thomas Brakell Ltd, 1891)

Birds Britannica, Mark Cocker & Richard Mabey (Chatto & Windus, 2005).

Buildings of Liverpool (Liverpool Heritage Bureau, 1978).

Charles Reilly & The Liverpool School of Architecture 1904-1933, Joseph Sharples, Alan Powers & Michael Shippobottom (Liverpool University Press, 1996).

C.J. Allen 1862-1956: Sculptor and Teacher (University of Liverpool Art Collections, to accompany exhibition in 2003).

Classics: A Very Short Introduction, Mary Beard and John Henderson (Oxford University Press, 1995).

Design Culture in Liverpool 1880-1914: The Origins of the Liverpool School of Architecture, Christopher Crouch (Liverpool University Press, 2002).

The Illustrated History of Liverpool's Suburbs, David Lewis (Breedon Books, 2003).

Liverpolitana: A Miscellany of People and Places, Peter Howell Williams (Merseyside Civic Society, 1971).

Liverpool: A People's History, Peter Aughton (Carnegie Press, 1990).

Liverpool City of Architecture, Quentin Hughes (Bluecoat Press, 1999).

Liverpool Heritage Walk: Illustrated Companion Guide, Liverpool City Planning Department (Liverpool City Council, 1990).

Liverpool – Maritime Mercantile City: Nomination for Inscription on the World Heritage List, Liverpool World Heritage Liaison Committee (Liverpool City Council, 2003).

Liverpool Roundabout, Richard Whittington-Egan (Philip, Son & Nephew, 1957).

Liverpool's Historic Waterfront: The World's First Mercantile Dock System, Nancy Ritchie-Noakes (Merseyside County Museums & Royal Commission on Historical Monuments, 1984).

Liverpool: The First 1,000 Years, Arabella McIntyre-Brown & Guy Woodland (Garlic Press, 2002).

Patronage & Practice: Sculpture on Merseyside, ed Penelope Curtis (NMGM & Tate Liverpool, 1989).

Pevsner Architectural Guides: Liverpool, Joseph Sharples (Pevsner, 2004).

Public Sculpture of Liverpool, Terry Cavanagh (Liverpool University Press, 1997).

Seaport: Architecture & Townscape in Liverpool, Quentin Hughes (Bluecoat Press, 1993).

The Story of Liverpool, F.A. Bailey & R. Millington (published by The Corporation of The City of Liverpool in 1957 to commemorate the 750th anniversary of the signing of Liverpool's First Charter by King John).

The Story of the Mersey Tunnel officially named Queensway (1934, reprinted in 1994 by Merseytravel to commemorate 60th anniversary).

The Streets of Liverpool, James Stonehouse (1869, reprinted by Liverpool Libraries & Information Services in 2002).

Transport in Liverpool, Adrian Jarvis (Ian Allan, 2001).

Underground Liverpool, Jim Moore (Bluecoat Press, 1998).

Walks Through History: Liverpool, David Lewis (Breedon, 2004).

Well, I Never Noticed That! The Decoration of the Buildings of Liverpool & Bootle, Parts 1 & 2, Andrew Richardson (West Derby Publishing, 2004).

BYGONE
LIVERPOOL

INTRODUCTION BY
RAMSAY
MUIR

LIVE
TOWN
1550